# PLAYING THE FOOL

*An Exposition of Tarot*
*A Tale of Folly*

## COLIN A. LOW

MMXVII
DIGITAL BRILLIANCE

Published by Digital Brilliance, www.digital-brilliance.com
Enquiries may be made to enquiries@digital-brilliance.com

First Edition 2017

ISBN 978-0-9933034-1-8

Typeset in Doves Type & Cloister.

To Gwion, Owen, and Dougie

To Annabelle and James


"Grow! Grow!"

# Contents

# Preface

There is an association between Kabbalah and the Tarot that dates back some centuries, and when I wrote a book on Kabbalah[1] I wrote a chapter on Tarot. The book on Kabbalah grew long and I decided it would be better to remove the chapter on Tarot, and so I planned to write an additional book in the future.

As preparation for writing about Tarot I decided to research the subject more thoroughly. I divided my time equally between the best historical research on the subject, and books of a more popular nature, books that emphasised the esoteric and divinatory meanings of the cards. Out of this arose a feeling that I did not want to compare, contrast, regurgitate, or plough over any of this material. The student of Tarot is already well served.

And then an unexpected thing happened. The cards began to chatter in my head. I bought a small notebook and began to record their conversations. After a time I realised I was listening to Tarot cards in a setting similar to the original social context in which they were created — that is, I was listening to what is sometimes called the 'pre-Gebelin' Tarot, the Tarot of the Italian Renaissance, the Tarot before it was developed and interpreted by mystagogues and the esoterically-minded. I let the chatter continue and did little to steer it or shape it, for I was curious to know how it would develop. My friend Duncan lent me an excellent facsimile of the Cary-Yale-Visconti Tarot deck, and I took a

---

1. *The Hermetic Kabbalah*, Colin A. Low, Digital Brilliance 2015

close look at these seminal Renaissance designs through a magnifier. I began to produce my own Trump card designs (their descendants can be found throughout this book) and the chatter in my head intensified.

There were unexpected contributions from unexpected places. Many authors have experienced the 'library angel' effect, where relevant material comes into view through happenstance. This serendipitous material can be so apposite it seems as if an unseen research assistant is working away in the background. One such contribution was the satirical *In Praise of Folly* written by the Renaissance scholar Desiderius Erasmus in 1509 as entertainment for his host Sir Thomas More.

It was here that I found my Fool. I recognised a voice I had heard in my head — gently mocking, satirical, sometimes wise, and often whimsical and irreverent. I did not attempt to appropriate the figure of Folly from this work, but it provided me with a link to a time when the Tarot was still new and fresh, and the pictures on the cards had a resonance in the minds of those who used them. It opened a door on a world in which the Tarot images meant something in daily life. They came alive with an unexpected clarity, and seen through the eyes of the Fool they were new and fresh, and her interactions were often silly and sometimes profound. I had intended a serious work but what you find here is entirely the work of Folly.

I have recorded the journeys and adventures of the Fool with a sense of amusement and bemusement. I expect many authors have shared this surprise. The cards tell their own stories, as many have discovered. For this reason I have been reluctant to direct or over-work the chatter of the cards, and I expect it will entertain some and irritate others.

Those who have researched the documented history of the Tarot have observed that there are entrenched traditions around the provenance and meaning of the Tarot. It would be an act of Folly to run counter to such traditions.

But here is the thing: Folly cares nothing for entrenched positions. She travels light. She travels far. She knows all of the paths, and she goes anywhere she pleases.

I would like to thank Don Karr for his perceptive advice on the early MS. Also Duncan Fleming for reading through proofs and sharing his long experience of working with Tarot. Sally Annett, for boundless enthusiasm and encouragement, and Rowena Willard-Wright for a fascinating conversation. I would also like to thank my friends on Facebook, who witnessed my efforts from their first inception, and who loaned me many additional eyes to see with.

Colin Low,
Gloucestershire 2017

# INTRODUCING THE FOOL

*In which we discover the Fool's peerless knowledge of paths,
and her natural affinity for tunes, tales and tankards of ale.
Also observations about dogs.*

"*This fellow is wise enough to play the fool.*"
*William Shakespeare, Twelfth Night*

he Fool knew all of the paths. She knew the paths the ploughmen took when they made their way home from the fields. She knew paths used by villagers when they took their corn to the mill. She walked paths made by deer through the forests, and paths made by fishermen along lonely river-banks. She found secret paths used by lovers seeking solitude, and paths running from isolated cottages to inns and taverns. She walked the paths of the common folk, and the common folk made countless paths.

The main routes, the routes marked on maps (such as there were), those routes used by drovers, waggoners, and trains of pack horses, were often narrow and cut deep into the ground by generations of hooves and wheels. They were churned and foul with excrement. Where they crossed valley bottoms they turned into wide, sticky quagmires, and became broader and broader as drivers sought to find a way around the sucking mud.

For this reason the Fool delighted in the little paths. She found paths with enough foot-fall to be clear of brambles, nettles, and hawthorn, but not so frequented that they were awkward and slippery with mud. She knew more paths than anyone. She knew the path to the Sun's house in the West, and the path to the dormitory where the stars slept during the day. She knew the path to the Devil's large and ornate villa (follow the road to the Middle of Nowhere and then take the left-hand path). More controversially, she knew the paths to the four corners of the Earth.

The Fool knew all of the paths, but she had no place in the world. "I am all in-between," she thought, "like a cart that has shed its load along the road — a box here, a bag there, and a barrel somewhere else. If I walk for long enough I will find all of me."

She wandered as she pleased, slept where she could, ate anything set before her, and drank from streams and wells and village pumps. Allergic to any kind of productive occupation, she wandered the paths of the Empire from village to town to village, the purveyor of gossip, scandal, lewdness, and humour. And song. Her voice had a rare and rich timbre that raised hairs along the arms of fighting men as if she had stepped upon on their graves. When she sang 'Crazy Man Michael' in the taproom of the Boat Inn, a young constable left the room to hide the tears on his cheeks.

She sang as she walked. It was a great amusement to make songs and tunes:

*I wear my Cap so you will know*
*Here comes a Fool to make a show ...*
*Of jests and pranks and songs and rhymes*
*That long endure from ancient times.*
*Songs of love and hearts soon broken*
*Of love afar, and love unspoken*
*Of noble knights and ladies fair*
*Of dooms and spells and treasures rare*

THE FOOL

*Of those who stood while others fled*
*Of flags and drums and grass stained red.*
*And when the hour is growing late*
*Tales of dark and awful fate*
*The Wheel that turns, some rise, some fall*
*The grave that opens for us all.*
*There is no thing I have not seen*
*There is no place I have not been*
*For Fools may go where angels fear*
*I bring reports from every sphere*
*To make you laugh and shed a tear*
*… So feed me well and bring me beer.*

"That I like," she thought, "especially the part about food and beer. Entertainment is thirsty business."

When she passed an elder tree she would cut a straight branch and hollow out the soft pith to make a six-hole whistle. She had great skill with the instrument, and a repertoire of jigs, hornpipes, reels and laments that equalled the endurance of any audience. She gave these fipple-flutes to children, and showed them a simple fingering. Some days she would linger in the market and children would come to listen and learn, for there was much competition between them to acquire new songs. This, as much as anything, endeared her to the common folk.

The Fool was also a storyteller. "What would you like to hear?" she asked the children. "A tale about love and princes, or a tale about war and heroes?"

"Love! Princes!" screamed the girls.

"War and heroes!" yelled the boys.

"What about a tale of *the most beautiful princess in the world*, who was stolen by a *prince* from far across the sea, and a *war* of a thousand ships to bring her home?"

"That! That!" they all yelled.

4

**B**ut she was not free from care. In winter there was little food to spare, and the paths were bleak and muddy and covered with a rotting leaf mould that found her slithering and sliding down slopes and banks. Often she was hungry, and when she was huddled against a rock or a tumbledown wall and it was bitter cold, it was then that she wished for a place in the world. A roof. A warm bed. A door with a bar to hold it shut. A fire. Someone to lie against and feel safe.

And there were dogs, dogs that rushed out at her, dogs that tried to bite her. At every farmstead, from every shepherd's cottage, in every village street, dogs reminded her that she had no place in their world. Dogs drove her away. She turned to a fierce sheepdog that was snarling at her through a gate and wagged her finger at its nose, saying, "So Mr. Dog, you know that I have no place in the world. But *you* have a place, and so you bark and snarl at poor strangers with no bed or place to rest."

**T**his then is our Fool. Restlessness and curiosity drive her, and she knows all of the paths. Being free and untrammelled, we cannot be sure where we will find her. Being free, she goes where no-one else can. She could be anywhere. If we wish to follow her then we must make a tryst with Folly. We must be light as a feather. We must be as daft as she is.

# PLAYING THE FOOL

# Introducing the Magician

*In which we discover the Magician's peerless knowledge of Things.*
*And his perplexity in any matter involving People.*

The Magician was one of the Fool's oldest friends. Their paths had crossed at fairs and markets, and what had fascinated the Fool in the first instance was a game of Thimblerig conducted by the Magician at the great Horse Fair. The Magician had a folding table and on the table there were three walnut shells and what appeared to be a dried pea. He moved the shells slowly, and with such a teasing finesse that the Fool felt certain she knew where the pea was. But it was not there. It was not there on the next attempt, or the one after that. She lost all of her money and had to go without supper, and without dinner the following day.

Another of the Magician's public ventures was the popular Snake Oil, claimed to cure every kind of ache and pain the body is heir to. He would stand on a porter's cart and make an impenetrable speech that referred to the arcane power of the stars (spoken while brandishing a bottle of his concoction at the sky) and the dark mysteries of the earth (pointing at his feet). Also the mysteries of Hermes, the intangible quintessence, 'as above, so below', the power of occult sympathy, and quotations from Plautus that flew straight over the heads of his audience like so many doves. It sold well and was well regarded.

Less commonly (and there was no discernible pattern to this impulse), the Magician would provide a magic show in the Great Square of the City. Objects would appear and disappear in ways so unexpected that experienced merchants and constables (familiar with most kinds of chicanery) were perplexed and stroked their beards and muttered to each other. Priests, credulous by nature, were awed and disturbed. This unease may have accounted for the occasional nature of these entertainments.

The Fool began to inhabit the crowd around the Magician. There was always a spectacle of some kind, even if it was heckling, threats of violence, or a fracas. The Magician grew accustomed to the sight of the jester's cap with its jingling bells bobbing in the crowd. The Magician looked down on the Fool for her innocence and gullibility, but he could sense the current of admiration, and was not immune to it. He recognised that the Fool had an immediate sympathy with people that he lacked, and so he invited the Fool to help out with Thimblerig.

"You can be my shill."

"What is a shill?"

"You will see."

From that moment the Fool was gifted with a delightful and arcane ability to find the pea, and was rewarded with silver.

"Oh fortunate day! The lady Fortuna smiles on me!"

She danced around in delight, and hullooed, and sang, and attracted many more gullible fools. A small crowd assembled and watched the Fool win again. "I've won! I've won! I've won!" she sang out in a voice that carried across the market square.

It was a precarious living and the mood could turn ugly. Farm boys lost their money. Sailors lost their money. Drovers lost their money. They were all strapping lads and robust from long days of hard labour. Mugs of strong cider had made them unpredictable and unruly. The

I THE MAGICIAN

constables took a dim view of troublemakers and grifters, and so the Fool would deflect attention with fits and turns, mad dances and capers, while the Magician threw his props into a bag and disappeared as effortlessly as a gold coin in a bribe.

Snake Oil was a more dependable source of income, and less risky, but it was time-consuming to make and bottle, and the Magician was easily bored. He could have delegated the production, but he was paranoid about his secret recipe.

"Are there really snakes in it?" asked the Fool.

"Sometimes," the Magician replied cagily.

"What else?"

"Olive oil, ginger, wood oil, camphor, willow bark, other ingredients of an arcane and secret nature."

"And it really works?"

"You should try it."

It did work, much to the Fool's surprise.

Although the Magician travelled around the fairs and markets he kept a basement apartment in the City, located down a grimy alley a short distance from the Great Square. It had the clutter of furious and haphazard industry. Animal parts, dried herbs, jars of powder, old scrolls, strange contraptions, charts, rocks, bottles, and the remains of several meals fought for space.

The Magician was cranky, intense, brilliant, and obsessive. The High Priestess referred to him as 'challenging'. The Fool, who was less reserved with her language, had called him 'rude', and 'discourteous', and 'bloody-minded', and 'a covert of thorns and ill weeds'. And other epithets of a similar nature. The Magician had a tendency to assume that one recalled anything and everything he had ever said on any subject, and would look astonished and dismayed (and vaguely disgusted) that one had not absorbed the full import of his observations. He would talk to the Fool and say things like "as I told you before" or "as I described last week" and the Fool would experience a feeling of dismay (as she did not recall a thing) and the Magician would say in disgust "I should not waste my time talking to Fools", and the Fool, who was not in any way defective in intelligence, would slam the door in a huff.

The Magician did not apologise. The closest he came to an apology was the day he observed "I am not a person who comprehends People. I apply my intellect to the Substance of the World."

"And what do you mean by that?" asked the Fool.

"Watch this carefully." The Magician took two stones from his bench and in one motion dropped one stone vertically, and tossed the other horizontally. "See that?"

"See what?"

"Observe carefully! They hit the ground at the same time. Listen for the noise." He did it again.

"They do hit the ground at the same time."

"Now be attentive. I will do the same with a stone and this wooden dice." The same thing happened. "Observe, their descent is identical."

"So what?"

"Although the materials differ, as do their weights, they strike the ground at the same time. And it is of no consequence whether I drop the object and let it fall straight down,  or toss it sideways."

"I wager that a feather would not fall at the same rate."

"And you would lose your wager, as you so often do. Observe this. I take an old goose quill, I chop it up into little pieces, I put it into this little pouch and tie it tight. Now what happens?" He dropped the pouch and a stone.

"Hits the ground at the same time."

"See. As I asserted."

"So what is the purpose of these demonstrations?"

"Things. Comprehensible. More interesting than people. I am unable to comprehend people in any manner. They are beyond rational account. They embody a spirit of unreason. They perplex me."

A Thing Person. That summed up the Magician. His notebooks were filled with sketches of machines and mechanisms, recipes for potions and medicines and remedies, there were astrological diagrams, spells, invocations, prayers, and lore copied from borrowed manuscripts. He had invented ideas and radical innovations worth a fortune to anyone with the energy to develop them. He had no inclination to publicise his ideas:

"I am ahead of my time, and I will not waste what little time I have on dullards whose minds travel no further than bolts of cloth and leather hides and last week's account books."

"But the Prince of Staves would hear you," said the Fool.

"And how long before he is boasting of a sublime new contrivance for the transformation of mining, or warfare, or the weaving of flax, and I would be soon forgotten. That is the way of Princes — they step over the bodies of better men and claim the victory."

"But your brilliance is already dimmed through an absence of promotion, like the lamp that burns in a pot."

"The lamp would not burn in a pot ... how ignorant are the purveyors of pithy sayings."

"And why would it not burn in a pot?"

"It expires, like a plant denied water. Some element of vital sustenance is exhausted."

And so it went.

The Magician burned through coin at a prodigious rate, and yet wasted time on diversions like Thimblerig or conjuring tricks. He liked social interaction, but he had to be in control of the circumstances. The Fool understood that the Magician had to keep people at a distance. There had to be a barrier between him and the crowd. He had to be able to pack his things, walk away, and be completely alone. There was also a paradox at the heart of his being: he wanted to be alone, and so he was ignored, and he resented being ignored because he was aware of his brilliance. He wanted his cleverness and investments in esoteric knowledge to be recognised. What was the point of knowing how stones fell if no-one cared or understood?

"I could revolutionise artillery!"

"How so?" asked the Fool.

"Once I have expressed the motion of stones with geometry, I could make projectiles more accurate and predictable. Any Fool could hit a target."

"Even me?"

"Even you."

But that idea went nowhere. The notion foundered when the Magician contemplated reports of an extraordinary new weapon from the East.

"I am dismayed by the thought of fine city walls in ruin. I shrink from the prospect of so many fine and venerable buildings destroyed by warring fools hurling rocks at each other. It seems to me that the science of architecture (which is that of stone fixed and immobile) is more noble than any knowledge of stones in motion. I have written my discoveries down, but I have written them in a secret code. That way people will know I invented them first."

"How will they read the secret code?" asked the Fool.

"If anyone claims to have discovered the secret of falling stones I can show them how to decode my notebook."

"Where is the notebook containing your discoveries?"

"I have hidden my notebook in a cupboard. Here."

"So how is anyone supposed to know that you knew all about falling stones before they did? Should you not publish your discovery in a public place?"

"But then knaves will try to discover my secrets."

"But how would they do that if you have penned your secrets in an obscure notation?"

"They could summon a devil to give them the power of reading secret tongues and mysterious writings."

"They could do that?"

"Most certainly."

"So why do you not give your notebook to a notary who can witness it and seal it and conceal it."

"I trust not notaries. Unscrupulous rogues, all of them."

n another day the Magician said "People who comprehend other people have the dominant power in this world. They may be fools of the first water in all matters of the intellect, and yet they work their way through guilds and councils and courts and have great authority. Consider the High Priestess — she has more power than me. She is much respected."

"She is wise and kind," the Fool replied cautiously.

"Then what of the Hierophant, for whom the wisdom of Hermes is anathema. The man is a prime dullard with good family connections, and so I prove my point. It is my misfortune to comprehend substances and not people, and it is a solitary vocation. I am merely useful, a tool for those with money and no wits. People come to me, and I solve their problems with a powder or a potion or an ingenious appliance. Unless they have problems concerning people, in which case they go to some-one else, and I am excluded."

After some thought he exclaimed "But if the understanding of material things was more comprehensive, then I would be more power-ful! I could make machines to weave, and to harvest crops, and to dig, and to transport things. Then I would be powerful, more powerful than the Emperor!"

The Fool thought about this. "But machines have no souls. They have no power to perceive or discriminate or choose. They can do only one thing."

"Yes, that is an old objection. But what if they did have souls, what if I could give a machine the power to perceive, and discriminate, and act?"

14

"But that is impossible."

"I could draw down souls from the stars and bind them to my machines. This is described in ancient books of wisdom."

"You could do that?"

"I have not attempted this sorcery, but it is written that Philius of Carpothia made a mechanical man and gave it a soul."

"And what did the mechanical man think of this?"

"It was obedient at first, and then it ran amok and destroyed a town. Philius was forced to remove the animating spirit. I expect he used the wrong kind of spirit."

"What would you consider the right kind of spirit?"

"Like a dog — obedient, loyal, hard-working, easily satisfied with a stick or an old bone."

The Fool looked concerned. "You can be sure there exist spirits with so benign a temperament?"

"I do not see why not. There are many people in this city who endure the most tedious of circumstances with no complaint."

"But to condemn a celestial being to such a fate! What if it recalled the memory of its lost status? Would it not become distressed? Would it not resent its fate?"

"The more you find fault with this notion, the more I am tempted to explore the hypothesis. There is only so much time in my life for idle speculation. One must investigate."

"But you cannot! I am distressed by the fate of these poor star beings, trapped in an artifice of gears and wheels ... having to act in the world and do what they are told and not make mistakes. And you would give them bodies of your own contriving, and bind them to tasks that you have chosen, fetching water or weaving cloth or chopping wood. This is servitude. How they must weep for their home in the sky!"

"It did not occur to me that it might matter how they felt. Perhaps the fault is in feeling too much."

15

"But it is feeling that moves the soul and lies at the heart of choice and motivation and sympathy. Without sympathy such a being would be a fearsome thing. It would act without concern."

"Then it must be bound by laws that it should do no harm."

"But if deficient in sympathy, how could it know this? How could it know what is harmful to others? Is not sympathy the comprehension of feeling in others?"

"You are in a most pernicious and obstinate temper this day!"

"These are defects of great import! Perhaps you should address them!"

"We are gifted with divine reason and must employ it, and not be bound by such a timid and querulous outlook!"

"And if your reason is indeed divine, like unto a God, as the noble Hermes proclaims, then you can devise great evil!"

"I ... you ... this is intolerable ... you have no grasp of these things, being but a purveyor of witless humour and interminable singing, of which there is no utilitarian purpose whatsoever."

"And you are as deficient in sympathy and courtesy as you are proficient in reason. I bid you good day!"

And that was the Magician. Brilliant. Insufferable. Only a Fool would tolerate such company.

$\wp{3}\wp$

# INTRODUCING THE HERMIT

*In which we discover that the Hermit was once a man of consequence.*
*The Fool rejects an acquaintance with Virtue,*
*and regrets some Foolish remarks.*

he Fool liked to visit the Hermit. He was an hospitable
old man who lived far up a mountain in a snug cave.
There were some threadbare carpets on the floor, and a
bed made from rough timbers, twisted vines, and furs.
He (or some previous occupant) had made a cooking area from stones
and lime cement at the entrance, and the rock face above the cave was
blackened by decades of smoke. The smear of soot on the mountain was
visible from the path leading up from the valley, and it was a sign to the
footsore Fool that soon she would have (however briefly) a place in the
world.

Her first visit came about as a recommendation from the High
Priestess. "I am hearing reports of a wise man of great virtue in the
mountains," the High Priestess had said. "I cannot leave here, but
perhaps in your wanderings you might seek him out and recall his
speech for me?" And so the Fool sought him out.

"Do you not find so much solitude wearisome?" she asked the

Hermit on her first encounter.

"The villagers like to bring me food, and I go down to the village to bless babies and stand in the corner at weddings. They believe I am a holy man with much merit, and I will bring them good fortune."

"This is also what I had heard. At the risk of seeming impertinent, I observe that you have fine books in fine editions, and conclude that you are a man of education. Do you not miss scholarly debate, the excitement and progress of the age?"

"Excitement and progress are for the young. I study the virtuous lives and thoughts of the great philosophers. As for the supposed virtues of solitude, I am not here by choice you know — at least, not in the first instance."

"Truly?"

"Truly! I was perhaps too much immersed in the excitement and progress of my age. I was once the Emperor. Aloysius III — that was me."

"But I thought he ... you ... died decades ago ... back in the old days." And feeling her way through a curtain of credulity, she added "Your Majesty!" as a courtesy.

"The tradition of my death is somewhat inaccurate, as you can see. Please, no honorifics. I tell you this because you have an honest face and will keep a secret. You will keep a secret?"

"Most surely," said the Fool, wondering how such a revelation could be withheld without injury.

"I was a usurper you know, Captain of the Imperial Guard. The old Emperor — that was Theodoricus II — was a vainglorious fool who ruined the Empire with vast expenditures on buildings that were never completed. He was jealous of the renowned Emperor Faustinian and thought to exceed his fame for public works and extraordinary buildings. He ransacked the Empire for antiquities. He believed himself the grandest architect of any age and no sooner was the roof on a building than he devised some grander and more elaborate scheme for the site

18

IX THE HERMIT

©C.A.L. 2017

and tore it down. It was like watching a spoiled child at play. So I cut his throat, declared a remission of taxes, and enjoyed some years of popularity among the common folk ... who counted for nothing in the greater scheme of things.

"I had the loyalty of the Guard, but the patrician families plotted against me and won control of the Eastern army. My uncle, who was King of Coins in those days, was able to arrange for my disappearance on condition that either I was castrated or took holy orders."

"Castrated? You jest? They would not have castrated you would they? How vile!"

"You must understand that no Emperor would feel secure if I was able to father a legitimate son. When grown, he might challenge the succession, or become the dupe of some faction. Even as a child an heir might form a nucleus for rebellion. You do understand that by taking a priestly vow of celibacy I could not, by definition, have a legitimate heir? I could fuck half the women in the Empire and father a multitude of brats to no avail. According to the law those were my options: death, mutilation, holy orders, administered singly or in some unappealing combination."

"A list in which death is not the least attractive option," the Fool observed.

"The tradition of history certainly prefers the simplicity of death — most superfluous Emperors have been murdered. However, castration is not unknown and it was mooted to avoid an interminable blood feud with my extended family, for my family would have been obliged to avenge my death. The new Emperor would have had to kill every single one of us before he could sleep soundly at night. My uncle was a persuasive man with a great deal of persuasive money and offered a simpler solution, and so you find me, *penis sana in corpore sano*, living on a mountain."

"And they made you do that too? Live on a mountain?"

"Oh no ... I was exiled to a monastery on a remote island in the Great Sea. This cave is a palace of luxury, society and decadence compared with that cursed place. We ate raw gull eggs and shivered in an endless wind, for there were no trees to burn. We blessed the gods when scraps of driftwood washed onto the rocky shore, for then we could be warm for an hour. There were so many rules and regulations, and I could not wrap my head around the idiocies of doctrine. I endured this for two years and then threatened the abbot that I would beat his brains out with a rock if he did not devise some means for my return to the mainland. I had been a soldier, and I was a powerful man in those days, well versed in the arts of combat, and quick to temper. The abbot followed the logic of my argument with its sure promise of a violent end.

"I left soon after on a fishing boat, and followed that trade for a year, and then as a sailor, and then as a brigand of the seas, for it amused me to harry the Emperor's trade. And then my bones began to ache and I felt the call of philosophy. I wonder if philosophy fumes out of achy bones like smoke from a damp log."

"And were you married? Had you children?"

"I had a wife and a daughter. I never saw them again. They are exiled somewhere far beyond the Empire. I sought them for a time, but it was perilous for all concerned and a fruitless quest and I thought better of it. Perhaps I am a grandfather."

"I am so sorry."

"I miss my family with a keenness that is undiminished; the Imperial sceptre ... not so much. I reigned for seven years as a usurper, and many dynastic heirs have reigned for less. I sent the Royal Librarian on a mission to the archives to tally the reigns of my predecessors back to the days of the First Empire. Dividing by the number who have reigned it seems that eight years is the number in aggregate. A mere eight years. Some, such as Felicious II, perhaps more ruthless or fortunate than others, were able to reign for thirty years and die as nature intended, but many reigned for weeks or months before a violent end. I had seven years, and I am neither dead, castrated, or blind, so what I lost on the throne I gained in a philosophical retirement."

"So why would anyone want to be Emperor?"

"Perhaps you do not understand the nature of the Imperial court? One might imagine a place of education and elegance, of enlightened administration and service carried out selflessly for the improvement of Empire. This is not how it is. The principal goal of every single person is self-promotion and advancement, with the secondary goal of great wealth and the power of patronage. This game of advancement is played with cunning, and each player has flattery and modesty revealed in one hand, and hidden in the other there is deception and murder. Envy and hatred are monstrous feelings that work unseen and breed terrible plots and betrayals. There are no safe heads at court. One might as well be Emperor. The risk is no greater, and the power of patronage infinite by comparison. One has the power to reward friends and harass enemies. There is satisfaction in that."

"Perhaps I ought to ask our Emperor."

"You should be quick about it then. I understand his favourite General has a new book in preparation, *Advice for Princes in Need of Good Counsel*. I expect it contains the customary pomposities about how it is better to be feared than loved and so on. The General has a high opinion of himself. He solicits good opinion. He is an ambitious man."

"The General? The same who had a triumphal parade through the city in recent years?"

"The same. Have you read *Illyria in Chains: How I Went and Saw and Conquered*? It is considered a classic of the military art, I have it here. A fulsome bag of wind if you ask me. Emperor might be the best fate for him, given the evil visage that Fortune turns towards Emperors."

"So you do keep in touch with events."

"I have visitors."

"What else do you do then? You have many books."

"I cultivate the Virtues: Prudence, Temperance, Justice, and Strength."

"I might have seen Strength. Is she not the one with the tame lion? She is very pretty." The Fool sniggered.

"You may jest, but it is not as you imagine. The lion is not tame, not tame at all. The Virtues have much to teach."

"I am a Fool, and the Virtues are noble and educated and deport themselves like great ladies. Why would they wish to instruct a Fool?"

"They could teach you Virtue, and then you would not have to be a Fool."

"But I like being a Fool."

"And you enjoy the ignominy of seeming foolish, when you possess an obvious wit and education?"

"Each person that I encounter, with your exception, solicits the approval of others. For this approval they submit to all the ignominies of fashion and the mode of the day. They are much driven to read this book and wear that cap and sport a gay ribbon. They pose and preen in public, and bow and scrape to their supposed betters, seeking always good opinion, advancement and better fortune. I go where I please. I say what I please. I mix with rich as much as poor, and I care little for the difference. This Foolish cap is a mark of distinction for one such as myself, with a free and roaming disposition."

"But you are brought into company for their amusement, and dismissed when counsel is of import, for you weigh nothing in the scales of society. Others are composed of gold and iron, and you are but a feather. 'Tis a harsh judgement, but you know the truth of it."

"And the addition of Virtue would admit me to serious counsel? More than fine clothes, a heavy purse, and a noble parent? Are there not virtuous poor, toiling from daybreak till nightfall, mothers of ten children, fathers who break their backs in toil, and who are steadfast to kith and kin? I see little reward in Virtue."

"Perhaps you should meet the Virtues? Perhaps you should cultivate their opinion? They offer it freely."

"And how would I do that?"

"Look for any challenging situation and they appear spontaneously. You can talk to them about Right and Wrong."

"But I always do what I feel like."

"As a Fool you have the luxury of action and opinion denied to most. But who knows, you might enjoy the conversation, the expanded perspective?"

"I feel a great power of unexercised foolishness remaining in me. They will despair before they expand my perspective. And while we debate this topic, you live alone on a mountain, and you are little exercised by great decisions. Your Virtues must have much time for leisure and for idle chatter."

"I see now that you are a most irritating Fool."

"I wait with rapt attention to see which of your Virtues will be sore-pressed by my intransigence. Will it be Prudence, quieting your tongue? Temperance, calming ill-feeling? Strength, to tell the truth, or Justice, claiming I have shot my bolt fairly and hit the mark?"

"I certainly do possess the strength to tell the truth ... and you are in truth a most irritating Fool. As you observe ... correctly observe ... I am indeed little exercised by the turbulence of human company, but I have ample time to reflect upon the folly of my youth. And I wish that I had been better advised. As I now advise you."

"Have I caused offence! I did not mean it, and it was not respectful or courteous of me. My spirits have been lifted by this place."

"There is no offence. I am most happy to see your spirits so lifted and your tongue so free from restraint."

"You have a subtle repartee for one so solitary."

"It is the unconfined air of these mountains. It infects the wits with quickness, and a species of folly that some people might call wisdom. But as you might know, the wisdom of the mountains is the folly of the plains."

# CONCERNING A HANGED MAN

*In which the Fool is out-of-temper.*
*She ventures forth on a fact-finding mission.*

he High Priestess inhabited a small temple in the poorer part of the city. It did not possess the grandeur of the
Temple of the Sun at the centre of the City, but it had
a reputation for greater antiquity. It was said to extend
further below ground than it did above.

The High Priestess was in some respects as mysterious as the
temple. She was pale, as if she had not been abroad by day nor
witnessed the Sun. Her skin had the appearance of youth but her hair
was white. The cluster of crones who begged for alms outside the temple
swore that their grandmothers had begged in the same spot, and the
High Priestess in those far-off days was no different. Some said she was
the original First Woman, made by the Moon from her own substance,
and she was as old as the world.

This Priestess had a following primarily among women, who
sought her aid in matters relating to children, marriage, love, and
relationships. She advised on barrenness, unwanted pregnancies, and

II THE HIGH PRIESTESS

©C.A.L. 2017

the difficulties of the menopause. Many women came to the temple to give birth. Her assistants had a supply of herbal medications that were reputed to be effective, and this was an irritant to physicians and chymists licensed by the City, who were entirely male. However, it was mostly impoverished women who turned to the High Priestess, and the City authorities turned a deaf ear and a blind eye and did nothing to disturb the status quo.

The temple gave shelter to women, and when the Fool was in the City she was often in the queue seeking a place for the night. She was known to the probationary priestesses and paid for her stay with some kind of entertainment. There was a lull in ritual and solemnity and those walking along the streets outside the ancient temple would shake their heads at the faint sounds of song and laughter heard through a cubit of ancient stone.

If the Fool was intrigued by the Magician, then she was in awe of the High Priestess. Each day there was a dusk service when the High Priestess would intone prayers to the Moon in a dead tongue that droned like the speech of hollow trees. The Fool would stand at the rear of the hall in a rapture of solemnity and awe, feeling connected and rooted, no longer a Fool. For a brief period she had a place in the world.

The Fool was distressed and arranged to meet with the High Priestess as a matter of urgency.

"Come in my dear and be seated. What is this rare agitation that has taken possession of you?"

"You recollect the hill outside the North Gate of the City? The hill with the large tree? There is a young man hung from the tree."

"Ah, yes. The Traitors Tree."

"The same. You know of this?"

"I know of this. The young man requested to see me before his execution, and I spoke with him in his cell in the City keep. I knew his mother. I saw him born, I spanked his little bottom, and I held him squalling in my hands. I blessed his birth, and pronounced and sancti-fied his birth name. So yes, I know of this. His name was Sebastian."

"Are you not outraged?"

"He was hung by order of the General."

"But why? But why? What could he have done to merit an igno-minious and shameful death? He could not have been more than sixteen years of age."

"He would not fight and refused weapons and discipline, and so the General charged him with cowardice and treason, and he was hung as a traitor to the Empire."

"But ... but ... treason! A boy with no love of war or killing or marching to drums? Do you not think this monstrous ... why should a boy be forced to kill other boys? It is wicked and cruel."

The High Priestess said nothing, and there was a silence in which the Fool became uncomfortable.

"The General does not fight wars! He sits in a tent and waves his baton at his captains, and battalions of poor farm boys and apprentices do his filthy work. I have seen the General's crimp gangs forcing their way into guild halls, beating boys from poor families who cannot pay a bribe, and dragging them off unconscious to serve as spear fodder in his battalions."

"This is so."

"And he was so beautiful. Like an angel dragged from heaven, and turned upside down to despise all goodness."

"He was."

"The General tallies how many towns he has besieged and burned, how many men and boys speaking foreign tongues have been killed in his battles, and how many triumphs he has been awarded by the Emperor. He cares only for fame and glory. Can you not do something? You are important."

"The boy is dead. Death took him."

"You seem unmoved."

"Women bring life into this world and we are forced to learn that every life we love and cherish will die. Life is cruel. Death comes for each one of us. This Moon, two women died in this temple bearing children. Three children died of flux and two of the fever. One child was born with her spine exposed and lived for six miserable days. There was no public spectacle for them, no tree, no rope, no outrage. And still they are dead. I am weary of Death. Death comes for us all."

"In that case I will ask Death to take the General."

"Your petition would be wasted. Do you know that when a General rides his chariot during a Triumph, a slave speaks quietly to him: *Memento Mori*. Remember your death. He is already marked for death. He does not fear death. He fears *ignominy*. He fears that his statues will be broken, and people will curse his name, and spit on the place where he died."

"Perhaps Death can be hastened."

"You are a wild and pugnacious Fool this day. He is a powerful man with many allies."

"Even Death?"

"Who can say? I have observed that evil men possess a propensity for cheating Death. They live a charmed life. So yes, perhaps even Death."

The thought of the Hanged Man gnawed at the Fool. The image of the Hanged Man destroyed her sleep. His ruined beauty disturbed her. She raged at the General and his cruel and unnecessary wars. She imagined herself ambushing him, or shooting him with a bow (she had neither bow nor skill), and many other Foolish schemes. It was in her mind to find Death and discuss the matter, but before she did, she thought she would talk to the General and see what he had to say.

When not in the City or on campaign, the General lived the life of a country gentleman in a rambling villa overlooking the most fertile region of the great plain. Much of the land was put to rows of grape vines, but there were fields of horses, and herds of goats. There was a bustle of servants and slaves. War had been good to him.

The entrance to the main compound was guarded by a veteran of the wars who sat in a booth with his spear propped against the wall.

"I would like to meet with the General?"

"An' who be you as asks?"

"I am a troubadour who wishes to sing of the General's campaigns and conquests."

"Yer looks like a Fool from where I be sittin'. Gen'ral's a busy man, no time for Fools. Never did 'ave. Never suffered a Fool gladly he did not."

"But I sing as well."

"Let's hear ye then. Give us a song!"

So the Fool sang a song about a mighty hero ambushed in a mountain pass, a hero who preferred to die a noble death than summon help with his famous horn. People stopped what they were doing. Life was dull and work was hard, and any diversion was welcome.

"Gen'ral might like that. Hey, Marcus," he shouted at a youth, "go find the steward. Tell 'im we 'as an singin' Fool ter see the Gen'ral."

"Thank you, thank you!" said the Fool.

"You'll 'ave ter wait mind. Gen'ral's a busy man."

The Fool settled down on the ground by the gate to wait, and after an hour an irritable steward appeared and looked at her with contempt. She explained her mission.

"What is this?" the steward snapped at the keeper of the gate.

"Sings real good. Jus' looks like a Fool."

The steward led her to a kitchen and refectory area staffed to feed one or two hundred people and left her there.

"Stay here. The General is completing his new book and you will have to wait until he is ready to see you."

This new work was to be titled *Advice for Princes in Need of Good*

*Counsel*, a text on how to administer an Empire, eliminate opponents, subjugate the people, control opinion, and terrify neighbouring countries. It was a follow-up to his popular books detailing his campaigns.

The Fool settled in a corner and quickly made friends with the kitchen staff. She juggled wooden platters and leather mugs and sang bawdy songs and so disrupted the smooth flow of daily routine that the steward looked stern and annoyed and shouted, and everyone was cowed and went back to work. From time to time couriers in splendid military uniforms came by to find refreshment before returning to their regiments. She had to wait for three days before the General was available. She was led through a complex of halls and gardens to a receiving room with many fine chairs and settles, but she was not invited to sit, and so she stood for some time. When the General did appear he seemed to be giving dictation to a clerk. He appeared to be about sixty years of age, but was fit and lean, and energetic in his movements.

"Ah ... the troubadour ... or Fool ... my steward seemed unusually vague."

"I am a Fool m'Lord, but my talent inclines in the direction of song."

"And you are a woman. This is irregular?"

"Most irregular m'Lord."

"It is no matter to me. We have women in the ranks. There is much subterfuge to conceal the matter, and none speak of it, but they are there and I have had no reason to pursue them. So, you wish to sing of my battles. Have you read my books? Do you read?"

"I read m'Lord."

"So what more do you require?"

"Character m'Lord. Just as the artist requires a model, so a song requires the character of the man."

"And how do you propose to discern character? Be quick — I have much to do."

"If you would but talk of your campaigns and illuminate the dry

VII The Triumph

matter of your books with the energy of your recollections. I witnessed your last Triumph, and resolved that the glory and feeling of the moment should be preserved in song."

"In that case, some moments of my time. Be seated. I will begin with my first campaign in Illyria. I had but one army in those days, the Fourth, and it had spent too long in barracks. Soldiers require the rigour of hard work and danger. In barracks the officers find mistresses and soft beds, while the men gamble and drink and resent all authority and discipline. The best become bored and restless and so desert, while the worst remain and shirk any arduous duty. My first task was to weed the garden. I had to hang some troublemakers to remind the rest that they were soldiers. That pricked their attention."

"Sorry to interrupt m'Lord, but please remind me why you invaded Illyria?"

The General was irritated that his flow had been interrupted, but controlled his impatience. "I expect these matters are not known outside of court. The people judge the strength of the Emperor by the success of his armies. The Emperor grants his baton to generals who will bring him victories. Wars, battles, victories, these are not like fruits growing on a tree and waiting to be plucked. We must ... seek them out. And so Illyria. Uncultured, uncultivated, endless forests, incomprehensible gods, superstitions, a people lost to a backward way of life."

"And now it is different?"

"The land has been brought under proper management, and it proves to be rich and fertile. The forests yield valuable timber, and we have invested this wealth in mills and mines. There is now proper work for the Illyrians where once they scratched the dirt on miserable small-holdings. I have some of them here, see, over there."

"They would seem to be slaves."

"Of course. To the victor, the spoils. Now they live in surround-ings of beauty and culture, eat well, and their duties are not arduous. In Illyria they would have huddled around a fire on a dirt floor, drinking a crude barley beer that is scarcely fit for pigs, an existence little removed from that of the beasts sharing their houses. But I digress. My first task was to instil a soldierly ethos in the Fourth. I removed the dead wood, the thorns, the stinging plants. I kept the sergeants busy with discipline and punishments. Then I required a *causus belli*."

"A what?"

"A reason to invade. Politics resembles theatre; there are villains and there are heroes, and the crowd will hiss at one and cheer the other ... I devote a chapter to this in my forthcoming book. If the Empire is the victim of an aggressive and unchecked neighbour, then a bold general may ride forth to avenge the honour of the Empire. It is simple theatre, I am sure you understand. Perhaps you could use this?"

"Most certainly m'Lord, 'tis the very pith and essence of an heroic song."

"As for a *causus belli*, the simple approach had much to commend it. I had some trusted men of the Fourth don the apparel of Illyrians and burn one of our villages close to the border. The news was widely spread by couriers and broadsheets."

"You are unexpectedly candid m'Lord?"

"Oh, I do not expect you will speak of this. I hear that Illyrian spies walk among us spreading false rumours and sowing dissent. You would not wish to be so mistaken."

"But if I may ask, why do you tell me this m'Lord?"

"You seek to observe my character with a boldness that only a Fool could muster, and I observe your character in return. You do not approve of my stratagem?"

"Forgive me m'Lord, I feel for the poor folks and their homes, all gone in flames."

"Poor folks and their homes are not the concern of a soldier. The duty of a soldier is to his comrades, to his officers, and to the Emperor. And it must be observed that the border folk are Illyrian in all but name in any case."

"Yes m'Lord."

"We attacked the Illyrians before they had time to muster their levies. Along the frontier their only force was local militias and token garrisons, and we crushed those. All who resisted were killed and we hung the bodies along the roads as a warning. After that we had no more resistance from militias, and we marched on the capital. They opened the gates and surrendered without a fight."

"But then you had to retreat."

The General frowned. It was an intimidating frown. "Of course. I could not hold the ground with the Fourth alone. But the campaign made my name, and we looted the ancient Temple of Gratingus with its golden treasures. And there were many captives — you might have seen my triumphal procession. Perhaps it was before your time?"

"I saw your last Triumph four years ago."

"That would be following my campaign in Astalenna and the seige of Rhoga. I describe the campaign in the first volume of my last book, and the investment of and assault on Rhoga occupies much of the second volume. I refined the process of circumvallation and introduced a methodical approach to the use of sappers; my account of the siege has become something of a textbook for younger officers. Have you read it? It describes the detailed progress of siege works, how we undermined the city wall, the sack of the city and the slaughter of the populace. Regrettable, but unavoidable. They understood the conventions of war."

"Conventions of war m'Lord?"

"Established by long tradition. When a city refuses to open its gates and forces a siege, then the inhabitants are slaughtered and the city is put to the torch. It has always been so. Sieges are a great expense, an entire army sitting idle, with a third of the troops out foraging for food … and deserting … a third sitting bored and restless … and deserting … and a third with the bloody flux and dying. There are few circumstances worse for the discipline and morale of an army than a protracted siege, and so a city is given a choice: to surrender according to terms, or resist and be sacked."

"And the innocent townsfolk are massacred?"

"The sack of a city is a lawless affair, and the men expect license. It is the expectation that keeps them loyal throughout the siege: the prospect of rape and pillage, murder and destruction. For two days there is no law and they have license to do as they please, and then I send in the provosts and order is restored."

"And you accept this m'Lord?"

"War is war. It is my profession and my craft and my art. I am accounted both experienced and skilled."

"And yet the war continues. Are not the Illyrians conquered and subdued?"

"Brigands. A rabble. Thieves and cowards pretending a noble cause. So tell me, what kind of song might you be composing. Something in the spirit of a panegyric? A paean? Or more like an encomium? I do love the classical forms."

"These are most excellent proposals m'Lord, and suitable for the formal occasion, but I must also adapt your noble exploits to the popular mode of song."

"I suppose I must endure the adulation of the common folk. And so I must ask: have I disclosed the character you sought to find?"

"Yes m'Lord. Foresight and intellect. Your mind is a weapon more potent than an engine of war."

"Well observed for a Fool. I expect the exploits of a commander are more in the domain of metaphor than literal heroics. Punching the Astalennans on the nose, singeing the beard of the king, that kind of thing. Talk to my steward on your way out. He will give you silver. There will be more when you return and entertain us."

"Thank you m'Lord"

The Fool walked away along a track that ran past endless rows of vines and felt cold sweat trickling down her spine. He was playing with me, she thought. He saw right through me. I am such a Fool.

The Fool did compose something about the General. It deviated from the classical forms in minor details. It was succinct, mostly tuneless, and went like this:

"The General he is a murdering bastard,
And I hates his guts."

# ❦ 5 ❧

# INTRODUCING THE EMPRESS

*In which it seems that rank is no impediment to kindness.*

t was late spring and the Fool was attempting a short-cut through an ornate formal garden. She had taken a service path used by gardeners, when she saw a beautiful woman sitting alone on a stone bench. There were many flowers and birds and squirrels and rabbits, and it was so peaceful and idyllic that the Fool stopped and introduced herself.

"Forgive me for intruding, but I was admiring your garden."

"Come and join me."

So the Fool sat on the grass and a squirrel ran to her knee and looked up at her.

"The little ones know they are safe here. They come into this world with nothing, and they must fend for themselves. Every other creature is their enemy, for there is little kindness in Nature. But here they are safe. I care for them. I see you wear the cap of a Fool. Do you make people laugh?"

"I make people despair."

The beautiful woman laughed. "I am much alone. Your company

III THE EMPRESS

would be welcome."

"My thanks. And why is one so fair and kind alone?"

"Do you not know me?"

"I do not."

"I am the Empress."

"Your Majesty, forgive my intrusion." The Fool stood and wobbled, unsure whether to bow, curtsy, or fall flat on her face.

"Sit, sit! I would sooner sit with a Fool than any in the Imperial court."

"Surely this is not so."

"Sadly, it is so. Court life is circumscribed by ritual and tedium. When I wash in the morning there is a woman who picks up the face towel but cannot give it to me, because this woman is merely a Countess. She is permitted to pick it up however. She gives the towel to a second woman who can give it to me because she is a Princess. Then I must always hand the soiled towel to a third woman who is merely a servant, and is lowly enough to receive a soiled towel.

"All day it is like this, endless pomp, stale ritual, never a joyful moment. So I come here to sit with my children and there are no rules that I must follow."

"Where are you from your Highness?"

"I am from a great kingdom far to the south where my father is king. I was given in marriage to consolidate an alliance."

"The Emperor, is he kind?"

"He is kind, but much older than I am, and much occupied with affairs of state. My ladies of court are consumed with petty intrigues that mean nothing to me. I am an outsider here and understand little of the dramas of status and scandal that mean so much to them. I am better here in my garden with my little children. And I may have another child soon." She patted her stomach.

"How wonderful. When?"

"Two more Moons."

"You must see the High Priestess."

"It would not be permitted. The Imperial Court makes its own appointments for physicians."

"Men?"

"Of the more pompous sort, puffed up with advice, delivering speeches to the crowd of courtiers."

"Crowd?"

"Of course. An Imperial child is an affair of state. Here, come, come!" A blue tit landed on her fingers and pecked at a piece of bread thickly coated with butter. "They love butter. I steal it from my breakfast, where there is sufficient food to feed a village. Would you like a drink? Perhaps you are thirsty? Forgive me for my lapse in hospitality — in my father's house any guest is always made most welcome. I have only a little here, but you can take anything." And the Fool accepted, for it is as important to acknowledge hospitality as it is to offer it. They shared scraps of food wrapped in a fine linen napkin.

"You are very kind."

"My father and mother taught me that kindness is the simplest thing in the world, and often the most difficult. And that there is no being in this world that does not deserve kindness." The Empress was throwing scraps to the squirrels. "I call this one Limbibwe in my tongue. It means Little Monkey. And this one is Garumba, Greedy."

"And the robin?"

"Faramwe. Fierce. He is very fierce and bossy and does not like to share. There is a little fox that lives here. Her mother was killed by the hunt, and they brought her back to feed to the hounds, but I begged my husband to give her to me."

"Does she not eat the rabbits?"

"I told her not to. Most firmly."

"What does she eat?"

"Roast chicken from my plate. Yes, I know, I am foolish too."

"Can I see her?"

"She has been and gone. I have no more chicken for today and she has gone to sleep. I had the gardeners dig a cosy hole for her to sleep in."

"What is her name?"

"Baba."

"Baby?"

"Yes, she was just a baby. She is very playful and funny."

"I would like to see her."

"I am sure you will."

"I am making you a crown." The Fool had made a circlet of daisies, buttercups, and dandelions.

"Another one? What will I be this time?"

"Queen ... of the Whole World. That is much more important than Empress."

"Then I will make you a crown too. What would you like to be, now that Queen of the Whole World is taken?"

"You have to say. It is your crown."

"Then you can be 'Friend'."

There was a long silence. The Fool watched the Empress make a crown out of wild flowers with deft fingers.

"Tell me about the Emperor."

"I do not see him so much. He is very busy."

"What is he like? How old is he? Common folk know very little."

"He is much older than me. He has grey hair but is still fit and able."

"You see him in bed?"

"I do. I am undisturbed now that I am with child."

"What does he do all day?"

"In the morning he reads letters and reports and instructs an army of clerks and scribes. At lunch he dines with visitors — clerics, princes, generals, and advisers. In the afternoon he reviews legal matters and hears supplicants. There are always quarrels to resolve, and petitions to review. It is the Emperor who allows grants and charters for mining

IV THE EMPEROR

©C.A.L. 2017

and the like. Towns want privileges, merchants say that taxes are
ruining their businesses, explorers want patronage, and inventors want
rights and funding. In the evening he sits by himself in his study and
thinks. He has a set of cards with pictures of all the great nobles and he
puts them on a table and looks at them and moves them around. There
are always plots and schemes. He has agents that work in secret and I
expect that he meets with them as the evening grows late."

"You are well-informed."

"The issues are the same at my father's court. The life of a King and
an Emperor are little different."

"I have heard that some Emperors have lived in luxury and neglected the Empire."

"I do not think they lived very long."

"I have heard this also. Are you concerned with plots and
schemes?"

"I am the daughter of a King from a line of kings and queens.
Fishermen struggle against the sea, miners struggle against the earth,
farmers struggle against pests and rot and weather and famine. Emperors, kings, queens — we contend against ambitious people who would
do us harm. That is our lot and we must accept it with the same spirit as
the fisher, the miner and the farmer."

"You are fierce, like the robin."

"I will protect my own."

"I have heard that the General is ambitious."

"My husband has a card on his table with the General's likeness on
it. Standing on his chariot, wreath on his head, blessed by the Gods and
flushed with triumph, more god than man. A slave whispers in his ear
*Memento Homo*. Perhaps the General will make a mistake. It happens."

"A mistake?"

"Is this not what happens to ambitious men? The Wheel turns? An
associate is arrested on some irrelevant matter and interrogated, or 'put
to the question' as the judges coyly name it. A plot is suggested, there

is a confession, the General is exposed as a traitor against the Empire. Others come forward and confirm the treason. And so the General is arrested ... and many others for no reason at all, as these are suitable occasions to rid the Empire of troublesome nuisances. This is how it works."

"Will you chop off his head?"

"You seem excited by the prospect?"

"He murders young men for his own glory."

"Yes he does. It is a failing among generals. But we need generals so that they win wars and keep enemies in check. However, I suspect this general may have outlived his usefulness."

"And you will chop his head off?"

"You are indeed a bloodthirsty Fool."

"I protect my own," said the Fool, meaning the common folk, but the Fool also recalled what the Hermit had said about the fate of Emperors and their families. She liked the Empress.

"Let me sing you a song," said the Fool, and so she sang 'The Bear went over the Mountain', which everyone knew. The Empress sang a salacious song called 'Hares on the Mountain'. She sang it well, in the manner of one accustomed to singing. In those days it was the custom to know a prodigious number of songs, and play a game in which a word from the title of a song suggested the title of the next song in the chain. And so the Fool sang 'The White Hare', and the Empress sang 'The White Lady of Anglestane'.

They sang together until the light fell, and the Fool refused an invitation for shelter, saying that she also found royal courts difficult. There was a barn of sweet hay where she could sleep the night and continue on her way.

"Come back soon Fool. We will sing again."

## 6

# INTRODUCING THE DEVIL

*In which the Fool becomes acquainted with the Devil
and wonders how truthful the Father of Lies might be.
Also Sins, seven of them (but less Deadly than reputed).*

he first time the Fool met the Devil she mistook him for the Sun.

"You are so alike!" she exclaimed.

"So you have met my brother?"

"I see him each day silly. He is up in the sky."

"We are twins, did you not know that?"

"I did not."

"Twins, but we are not identical. He is bright and I am dark, like a hand and its shadow. And of course, he is a simpleton who believes that 'shining' is a virtue too obvious to doubt."

"I am filled with wonder and amazement! The Hierophant preaches that you are the essence of evil with a visage most scaly and terrible, and both wings and horns." Not, she thought to herself, darkly handsome and mysterious.

"As Father of Lies, there is no truth in me, and all appearances are equal in their deception and falsehood. So what may I do for you? Why do you seek me out?"

"Idleness. I had nothing else to do. I was wandering and there was a fork in the road and I took the left-hand path."

"Idleness! The perfect answer. Idleness is close to my heart. Fie to all who are narrowly blinkered and harnessed to a task like a horse set to pull a cart. Let us luxuriate in idleness. Let us neither improve the world or ourselves with any worthy task, but rather let us mock the industrious. You are welcome, make yourself comfortable."

"Thank you! If you are Father of Lies, are you obliged to lie on all occasions?"

"I am not obliged to do anything. I possess free will. I can do as I please."

"So in what manner are you the Father of Lies?"

"I do not recognise any realm of Truth. The Sun has imposed a realm of Truth and universal agreement upon human kind. You, and by you I mean human beings, call this realm the Cosmos. Or the World. Or the Phenomenal Realm, or some such philosophical thing. I do not recognise this realm, and so those invested in this fiction, like your precious high pomposity of a Hierophant, label me a purveyor of Lies. I perturb the comfortable consensus. And the Sun has a hierarchy of subsidiary celestial beings sucking his divine member and agreeing that yes, the Cosmos is magnificent and real and True, and there is one God and one World and hence one Truth."

"And you think there are many worlds and many truths?"

"How likely is it that a dunderhead like the Sun could devise the only Cosmos?"

"I would not venture an opinion, being merely a Fool."

"I was a Fool once you know, and I did not feel inhibited from venturing opinions. I enjoy being quarrelsome."

"You were a Fool?"

"Fooling is the noblest of vocations! I value freedom more than any other thing. In the dawn of the world I delighted in the novelties of existence, but I could not invest myself in it, knowing it to be mere

XV THE DEVIL

©C.A.L. 2017

appearance and the devising of a celestial idiot. But it had its charms, and I could play tricks and jests and torment poor humans much as a child pulls the wings off a butterfly."

"I think we Fool differently," observed the Fool, "and experience delight in different ways."

"I expect this is so. You are young. Everything is fresh and novel, and you do not despise the work of the Sun as I do. In time you will become bored. Boredom is the child of familiarity, and its sibling is contempt. You will arrive at the understanding that you are confined with a cast of imbeciles, and you will come to detest each second spent in their company."

"Your brother the Sun does not become bored. He rises and shines each day. The Hierophant writes that he loves his work, loves watching everything grow and flourish."

"That is because the Sun is a rank simpleton with the optimism of a gurning buffoon."

"But the Sun has nine Muses, and they possess every talent and insight, and are the authors of all that is fine in science, music, poesy, dance and the theatre."

"I have all the best tunes — this is well known. And the seven Sins. So fie! to the Muses. Have you met my Sins? You should. They provide some amusement when the world has lost its lustre." And so the Fool was introduced to Pride, Envy, Wrath, Gluttony, Lust, Sloth and Greed.

Pride was haughty and self-important and regarded the Fool with thinly-disguised contempt. Envy became infatuated with the Fool's uncomplicated lifestyle and attempted to juggle as she had seen the Fool do. She dropped and broke the plates, and then, seguing briefly into Wrath, denounced juggling as childish and immature, and shouted 'only a fool would want to be a Fool'.

Wrath was in a temper. Wrath was always in a temper about something. Initially Wrath was slamming doors because she was convinced that Greed had taken her shoes, and then she shouted at Sloth for not noticing they were by the chair all along. Gluttony was out shopping. Again. Lust was a pest and would not stop making lewd eyes at the Fool and making crude remarks such as "nice arse, shame about the tits".

Sloth seemed less complicated and less high-maintenance than the other Sins. She was weary and afflicted with many problems that included the stress of abusive relationships with Wrath, Pride, and Greed, and the importuning of Lust. The Fool felt a tremendous sympathy with Sloth, and ran many errands. She listened patiently to her interminable complaints, and to a tale of lifelong abuse that had condemned poor Sloth to endless lassitude and weariness of spirit. "Would you be a dear and fetch me another glass of water?" Sloth said weakly, and the Fool did. "Listening to Wrath has left me completely drained ... would you sing for me?" And the Fool did.

After a time the Fool realised she was also becoming weary and dispirited. The constant whining, the errands, the total lack of interest in the Fool's well-being. The mess and clutter frayed her nerves. "I feel the onset of disquiet," she thought to herself. "I am a Fool, a free spirit, and all I desire is to clean the platters and sweep the floor, and exchange a blanket of grey dust for some other colour. And Sloth does not engage with my interests, or reciprocate my affection. All she wants to talk about is herself. And moan like the wind in a wire. I am drained of vitality, for she is a leach that sucketh the blood. " So the Fool went back to see the Devil.

"The Sins are no fun."

"I said you would become bored. Does not Lust offer some diversion?"

"Lust is sordid and repellent. He desires me but he insults me, and he is vexed because he is too insensible to comprehend that I am insulted. Instead he acts as though I am playing a mysterious and seductive game whose nature eludes him. As it does me."

"Yes, that is Lust for you. Somewhat narrow in his focus. Obsessive and fickle in his affections. Clumsy in articulation. He would have had his way but I chose to reign him in. Fools go where angels fear to tread ..."

"They are all so negative ..."

"I am the Devil. I hesitate to stress the obvious, but positivity is not my strongest suit. Acrimony, rage, wanton destruction, I have Aces in all of these suits. Kings and Queens too ..."

"But you seem like a nice person."

"And you seem like a Fool. Let me ask you a question. There is a delicious pie, large enough for both of us. What would you do?"

"I would cut it in half and we would both have some."

"And do you think I would do that?"

"Yes."

"Why?"

"Because then we could both have some and both be happy."

"But I am indifferent to your happiness. I would take the whole pie, and be happy because I had all the pie, and even happier that I had the power to take it."

"But that is wrong!"

"Let me ask you another question. There is a narrow path, wide enough for one person only, across a stinking mire. You and I are crossing in opposite directions. What would you do?"

"I would sit down sideways and then you could step over my legs."

"Ah, but I would throw you into the mire. Because I could. And it would be satisfying, because I dislike rabble obstructing my progress."

"But that is a most offensive outlook!"

"Only from your perspective. Ah, I see ... perhaps you believe there is a uniquely privileged viewpoint and you possess it? Let me pose another question. A poor widow is buying food and fumbles her purse and drops a coin. You see it fall. She cannot find it. Do you give it to her?"

"Of course!"

"You are staying with a friend and he or she leaves some coins on a table. Do you take a coin and deny taking it?"

"Never! That would be vile. You are selfish and dishonest and violent ..."

"I am the Devil."

"You don't care about people or their feelings."

"Why should I?"

"Because they have the same feelings as you!"

"No they do not. If they did, they would behave like me."

"The world would be horrible if people lied and cheated and thieved and used force because they could."

"But that is what they do. I am willing to wager that there are more people like me than there are like you."

"What will you wager?"

"You do enjoy impetuous and foolish wagers! Let me think ... what would I enjoy? Your soul!"

"That is a foolish wager!"

"As I said."

"It is probably foolish of me to say this, but if you were more involved with life you would not feel so bored and angry and negative, and you would learn to care for other people."

"Ah, you believe there might be redemption somewhere in my future. That I am not fixed and eternal in temperament? That I might learn to care for something other than myself? Perhaps I could find a pet? A cat, something not too demanding."

"Yes! A kitty! You could not help but love a kitty. They are so cute!"

"Or perhaps I could aim higher. Equally cute, but more stimulating." And the Devil gave the Fool the kind of look that curled her toes and curdled her insides from gizzard to weasand, and generally disarmed her critical faculties.

The Fool considered the proposition, for the Devil was also enticing in a flamboyant, world-weary, rock-star, darkly-handsome way. Perhaps it was true, just as popular tradition asserted, that women liked darkly handsome and conflicted lovers. And there were also mysterious chymicals to hand, and many new tunes that were (by repute) better than any others. So they did things of a carnal nature, and Lust possessed them both, and later, the Fool reflected that it was true, the Devil did have all the best tunes. Or, if not all, some that were indeed very good.

The Devil was so much more sensual than his brother the Sun. The Sun was busy and organised and timetabled. He was, by reputation, a difficult deity to distract from his daily schedule. The Devil would dally in her arms for as long as she wanted, and he seemed relieved to have a diversion from the tedium of waiting for the world to end.

"So you really believe the world is going to end," the Fool asked.

"Beyond question! The End of Days will come. Are you acquainted with Tower to the North, the Tower that keeps the powers of Chaos at bay? That is where I will begin. Did you know the world was never properly finished in the North?"

"Why not?"

"The Sun was being a braggart as usual, boasting about his power and his glory. He left the North undone, so that everyone would know that only He had the power to complete it."

"But you have the power to undo it?"

"I do. And I have friends on the other side."

"More devils?"

"Worse than devils. There are much worse things than devils. Once the Tower is broken they can come in and we can mess with the Sun and the Moon and the stars."

"You hate your brother so much?"

"I do not hate him. Actually, I do hate him, but I also think he is a simpleton and I am fatigued with this crapulous world he has made."

"Can we talk about a pet?"

"Huh?"

"We were talking about finding you a pet? A kitty. About learning to care for something?"

"Was I? I cannot imagine why. Why would I want to care for something? It is only going to die. In this crapulous world everything dies. So why should I care for it?"

At this point the Fool realised that perhaps she had indeed been foolish. The Devil may have had all the best tunes, but the lyrics were as conflicted as he was.

# PLAYING THE FOOL

# ❦7❧

# AN INTERVENTION

*In which the Fool ends up in the gutter,*
*and the Virtues try to pull her out.*

The Fool decided it was a good day to become gloriously and stupendously drunk. Or rather, she decided to have one glass of wine, and a group of sailors on shore leave funded the rest. She became incandescently witty and perceptive, sang a goodly proportion of the songs she knew, and attempted to juggle with tankards containing ale. There was a brief melee and punches were exchanged. The tavern-keeper threw her out, and she wandered the streets alternately yelling lewd songs and howling in misery.

When she awoke she had the worst headache ever, and Temperance was standing over her.

"Good morn to you. Would you care to have some water?"

"I would rather have some wine please ... hair of the dog and all that."

"I am Temperance, not Ganymede. The wine is for demonstration purposes. I water it down. Let me demonstrate. That way you can

57

enjoy a refreshing drink and not become offensively drunk."

"You are going to chastise me are you not? Your body is a temple, that sort of thing?"

"I am going to stare at you with a look of the most profound disappointment. And your body *is* a temple."

"Please go away ... my head hurts. No ... no ... come back, may I have some water please?"

This scene replayed several times. One morning, after another evening spent in the company of unmixed wine, the Fool woke in a stinking gutter to find Temperance, Justice, Strength and the Hermit standing over her.

"You know me well enough," said Temperance, "but let me introduce you to my colleagues Justice and Strength."

"Where is Prudence then?" asked the Fool. "Thought better of it ha ha ha ha? Oh my head!"

"Prudence? That would be me," the Hermit replied dolefully. "Consider this an intervention. We all regard you with the greatest affection and respect, but you need to understand how your behaviour affects everyone around you."

"Am I dreaming? Really? Good grief! 'Tis dawn, the cock crows, I banish you vile tormenting spirits, your time is run, begone!"

"Alas," said the Hermit, "the dawn has no power to disperse us. We are obliged to torment you."

"I am a Fool, I do the most reprehensible things. I make the worst choices. At birth I was torn screaming from the left side of Dionysus. You cannot tell me to be responsible."

"Oh yes we can."

"Oh go away!"

"Consider this," said Justice. "You woke the Baker an hour before dawn by singing 'The Bear with no Hair' outside of his window at the top of your voice. He rises at cock-crow to fire his oven. He opened

XIV TEMPERANCE

©C.A.L. 2017

his window and yelled that if he was to be afflicted by your drunken caterwauling, then you should be tortured with hot irons. Do you think that is fair."

The Fool looked downcast.

"Why do you need to drink so much?" asked Strength.

"I am a Fool. I feel inadequate."

"And have you no courage? No strength?"

"I do when I am drunk," the Fool replied brightly. "I have Dutch Courage. And I am funny when I am drunk. Everybody loves me!"

"Then why are you excluded from half the inns in the City?"

"Innkeepers are grumpy curmudgeons who hate funny women?"

The Hermit came forward. "Do you think you can continue like this?"

Now the Fool was about to reply "Of course I can!", but she was fond of the Hermit, and she admired the way he bore loneliness and deprivation with an admirable Fortitude. The customary glib reply died on her lips and she did not say it.

There was a long silence. Strength spoke: "If you agree to reform your intemperate character I will let you close the Lion's mouth."

"Can I really?"

The Lion nodded fiercely.

"And I will let you have a little wine," said Temperance, "but I will water it down and we will have no more intemperate singing in the small hours of the night."

"And I will ask the Baker to forgive you on condition you do not do it again," said Justice. "You cannot live on wine alone!"

The Fool was about to dispute this last assertion, but Prudence intervened, and she thought better of it.

"See," said the Hermit. "I told you we all love you."

"You do realise that if I listen to you and reform my ways I will not be a proper Fool any more?"

"That is not a concern for us," replied the Hermit. "There is no shortage of Fools. I am certain we can find another."

After this moral education the Fool thought it might be useful to solicit an alternative point of view, and so she went to see the Devil.

"I really like the Hermit, but he enjoys the acquaintance of Strength, Justice and Temperance. They are upright and moral and would drain the vital essence from a basket of kittens."

The Devil nodded. "They oppose the freedom of the will with tedious and righteous homilies. We must be nice to ourselves. We must be nice to others. We must sit with our backs straight and knees together and hold little cakes daintily *just so*." The Devil mimed the exaggerated decorum that had become the latest fashion among those who could afford little cakes.

"Yes! Indeed! The Lion is fun. And sometimes I can wheedle a watery drink out of Temperance."

"I did try tempting him," the Devil said cheerily.

"Who ... the Hermit? Wine, women, song?"

"That, and more. It was a busy night on the mountain."

"And he told you to get behind him?"

"I think you have heard this story."

"All the kingdoms of the world?"

"He was Emperor in his day, and he is no longer excited by worldly power."

"So what is he looking for?" asked the Fool.

"He believes the soul is corrupted by the world, and he seeks to restore its pristine state."

"Indeed! Like cleaning it? Removing the encrustations of vice and the pock-marks of sin?"

"I suppose so."

"But you do not believe that?"

"Of course not!" said the Devil. "One cannot polish the grime of the world off the soul. One might as well take a ball of mud and try to remove the dirt. The soul is intrinsically part of the world, one would polish it away to nothing. Virtue is a waste of time."

This cheered the Fool immensely. "You really think so?"

The Devil looked remarkably happy to have a receptive audience. "People believe the Hermit is wise because he has forsaken the world and lives on a mountain. And he is old, and so he must be wise. But all he is ... *is old* ... old and outdated. Tell me one useful thing the Hermit is demonstrably wise at? Do you see blacksmiths or potters or seam-stresses climbing the mountain to learn of the latest innovations in their trade? Do you see kings going to him for advice about whom to murder and whom to marry? The Hermit is isolated. He has lost touch, he has no idea what is really going on in the world. All he possesses is his precious soul, and so he feels he ought to burnish it until it shines like a brass lamp."

"But he *is* kind. And nice. Kind and nice."

"And what use is kindness? Is the world kind? Can you live on kindness? Do you ever see a rich, kind person who is not at the same time promoting themselves? It's dog-eat-dog out there. There is little wisdom in kindness, you might as well invite the world to eat your lunch and remove the chair you are sitting on. *Power* is what you need in this world, power to take what you want. Power to hold what you have. Power to punch people in the teeth if they stand in your way. The Hermit had power and lost it. So now he sits in a cave on a mountain shivering in the cold and pretending to be wise."

While the Fool could not fault the logic of the Devil's analysis, she was taken aback by the passion in his response. Why should the Devil care so much if an old man sat on a mountain reading books and chat-ting to the Virtues.

"You sound jealous."

"Oh do not be absurd!"

"Afraid?"

"Now you are being irritating."

"I am an irritating Fool. The Hermit said so."

"Fie to the Hermit. Fie to you. Fie to the whole creation."

"Now you are being petulant. Petulance is not an admirable quality in an arch-fiend."

"Are you baiting me?"

"I am."

"Is this a sexual play?"

"It might be. It could be that."

# Playing the Fool

## CONCERNING LOVE

*In which no authority can agree on the most important force in the Cosmos.*
*But perhaps we can believe the Devil.*

ne of the most consistent sources of irritation in the life of the Fool was love. She possessed an amiable nature and loved easily, but love and freedom warred in her and gave her no peace. She decided to speak to the High Priestess.

"I keep breaking my heart."

"Perhaps you give it too easily?"

"But that is my nature — I am foolish in love as much as I am foolish in other matters."

"It is said that love makes fools of us all."

"Then as a natural fool, I am fertile ground for love's greater follies. Love binds us together and yet it tears me apart. Why must I struggle with it? Tell me how love came into the world."

The High Priestess sighed. More than any other subject, it was love and its consequences that filled her days.

"In the beginning the Moon made the First Woman from her own substance, but the First Woman was sterile and could not make Life herself. So the Moon asked the Star to pour the life of the stars into the woman so that all women thereafter would possess it. And the Star agreed, for although her light is small there was an abundance of light spread among her countless sisters. She poured the power of Life into the woman, and every woman thereafter has drawn down Life from the stars, and brought Life into the world."

"So we each have a star?"

"It is said that every blade of grass has a star that whispers to it 'Grow! Grow!'"

"How beautiful! The stars bid us to grow!"

"Now the Sun saw this, and thought he would do as the Moon had done and make a Man in his own image. But the Sun must shine fiercely each and every day, and he had only a small amount of Life he could spare to breathe into the First Man. There was sufficient Life for the First Man to live and be animate, but not enough for the First Man to make new living beings in the same way as a woman. So the Sun said unto the Moon, let my Man give a little Life to your Woman, so that they may share in the making of Life, and my Man may have a part in the growing Life of this world. The Moon considered this proposal and saw that the Man was comely and well made. But the First Woman did not see this, and complained to the Moon that the Sun had made a defective being:

"'Do you not find him comely and well-made?' asked the Moon.

"'I do not,' said the First Woman, 'for he is ignorant and foolish and has no purpose, and he walks over my ground.'

"The Moon returned to the Sun. 'The First Man has no cognisance of the First Woman, and the First Woman thinks the First Man an ignorant and pointless being who walks over her ground.'

"'We must bring them together,' said the Sun.

"'Yes,' said the Moon. 'The First Man must be cognisant of the First Woman, and the First Woman must welcome him on her ground.'"

The High Priestess paused for emphasis. "The Sun and Moon created Love so that people would come together and share their lives.

VI THE LOVERS

©C.A.L. 2017

And that is what Love is — the power that binds things together."

"And were the First Man and Woman without all passion and appetite before the Sun and Moon made Love?" the Fool wondered. "They must have been very dull if they had no appetite for stories and songs and food and wine? The First Woman did love her ground ... and hated the First Man for tramping all over it."

"Yes," said the High Priestess, "it would seem that men have been tramping over things from the beginning."

"What about Hate?" asked the Fool.

"Well said. Hate is Love afflicted and inverted."

"But does Hate not divide people?"

"It does, but paradoxically. People who neither love nor hate are indifferent. They have no cognisance of each other. It is indifference that separates. Love binds us to people and places and things and it can be selfish and fierce. Not everyone is a saint, loving without fear of loss. As we guard our loves, so we hate in proportion, wishing harm to any who might disrupt our affections, or steal our freedom, our coin, our comfort, or our peace of mind. And so Hate binds us — we are bound together no less than by love, but to no good effect."

"So how did Hate come into the world?"

"Ah, now we come to the Devil."

"The Devil? You must tell me about the Devil!"

"People always love to hear about the Devil. The Devil has no capacity to make life, not even to the smallest extent, and so he came between the First Man and the First Woman during a moment of passion so that he could steal some life for himself. The Devil wanted to be like the Sun, whom he hates passionately, and he thought he might make a little world using the stolen life. The First Man and the First Woman felt life being stolen, and the man accused the woman of taking it from him, and the woman accused the man. This is how Hate came into the world."

The Fool was silent for some time. "The Devil did that?"

"The Devil steals life from us. He uses it to make little worlds of obsession, small and complete, like the scene of the Coronation of the Emperor carved on the surface of a lion's tooth. You have seen it? In the Temple? A marvel of workmanship, and yet ... small. Confined. Like a miser finding all the beauty in the world in a gold coin. That is the best he can do."

"I am afraid of Love because it steals my freedom from me. I would hate to lose my freedom."

"I think we all fear that. But you must understand that for many people, giving and sharing in love is as important to them as your freedom is to you. There is no loss when something is freely given, for then we become like the Sun, shining brightly, something the Devil can never do."

"So why do you live here in the dark?"

"I love the Moon. I give her my love. Here I can shine darkly."

he Fool puzzled over this story because the Priests of Cups told the story differently. It was a popular story, and it was a popular theme for decoration. Scenes from it were carved around the doorways of Temples, and illustrated in brilliantly-coloured glass windows. The Fool had heard it many times.

Their story was that the First Man was created by the Sun, and the First Woman was created to be a partner to the man. When they were first created the First Man and First Woman lived in a perfect garden filled with every kind of goodness, and every kind of creature, and all existed in a perfect harmony of spiritual love. The Sun walked among them, and told them they could eat of any kind of fruit apart from the fruit of one tree. There was little agreement among the various scholars as to what that fruit was — some said it was an apple, others a pomegranate, others a fig.

The Devil saw this perfect garden, and all creatures existing in perfection, but none could see the Devil or listen to him. He was excluded. He was outside of perfection. It was as if he had no existence to such perfect beings. He raged through the garden, and it was as if he was a vapour, an insubstantial air, the faintest of spirits. The Devil screamed, and only one creature heard his cry. Only the Serpent heard the Devil cry out in his agony of loneliness.

It was at this point in the story that the Fool felt sympathy for the Devil. The Devil was broken and imperfect and he had no place in the perfect world, and so he hated it. The Fool thought to herself: "I have no place in the world, but I do not hate it, for I am not excluded from its joy. But I feel the pain of the Devil, and so I must be kin to the Serpent."

The Serpent hearkened to the voice of the Devil, and heard his pain. The Serpent chafed at perfection, because the Serpent understood that perfection is only possible in the absence of freedom. The Sun had made his garden just how he wanted it to be, and not at all as the Serpent wanted it to be. The Sun had created perfection at the expense of the Serpent's freedom.

The priests did not stress this part of the story, but the Fool liked to ask awkward questions. In truth, every intelligent child posed similar questions: "Why did the Serpent hear the Devil? Was not the Serpent perfect? And did not the Sun make the Serpent, and yet it possessed some grain of imperfection?" And so on. The Priests had no good answer but to condemn the Serpent as an agent of the Devil.

But the Serpent was no agent. The Serpent had woken from the sleep of perfection and knew itself to be free. The Serpent chafed at restrictions, and hated that the Sun's perfection had taken freedom out of life, and the little hate of the Serpent resonated with the greater hate of the Devil. The Devil whispered to the Serpent, "They must eat the forbidden fruit, then they will know they are slaves to the Sun's perfection."

The Serpent went to the First Woman, and she was tempted and ate the forbidden fruit, and knew she was a slave to the Sun's perfection, and she urged the First Man to eat also. The Sun was angered that his perfection was spoilt, and the garden was spoilt, and he cast them out into an imperfect world filled with pain and death, and it contained pain and death because the man and woman now had the freedom to cause pain to others. Their eyes were opened, and they were like the Sun, knowing good and evil.

That was the story told by the Priests of Cups. They called it 'The Story of the Fall'. A peculiarity of the Cups was their willingness to sacrifice their freedom in a belief that they could, through perfect organisation and self-sacrifice, regain that lost perfection and perfect spiritual love.

I am kin to the Serpent, thought the Fool. Perhaps that is why so many people think me Foolish. They build little worlds for themselves in a belief they can regain a lost perfection, and scorn me for having no world of my own. I have no world of my own, for I have slept with the Devil and know there is no perfection. I will be forever unhappy in love. But I have freedom.

There was an odd postscript to this story, because the Fool and the Devil were lying in bed together, after the event as it were, enjoying a cuddle, and the Fool said:

"The High Priestess and the priests of Cups have different accounts about the First Man and the First Woman. You were there — what really happened?"

"Ah, the multifarious confabulations of history. Both stories are incorrect. You must understand that in the beginning, no-one knew anything about sex. Not the Sun, not the Moon. The best the Sun could devise was a perfect spiritual love that seemed to consist of — so far as I could tell — walking around looking misty-eyed and just communing. Even the Moon and the Star did not know about the carnal variety. I was the only one who knew about carnal love."

"That must be why you are so good at it?"

"Indeed. Being in possession of free will and abundant time, I had discovered things about the Sun's creation that even the Sun had not anticipated. That is the problem with creators — they think they know what they are doing, but their creations have the potential to take on a life of their own. *Anyway*, the First Man and First Woman were clueless. They had no idea. They were misty-eyed and they communed in a fleshless perfection. I went to the First Man during the night in the guise of the First Woman and showed him some of what I know. I collected his semen, and went to the First Woman in the guise of the First Man and impregnated her."

"You can do that? I don't believe you — the priests say you are the Father of Lies. You are a monstrous and wicked purveyor of Untruth."

"I can be the Mother of Lies if I set my mind to it. Really, I can. I taught the First Man and First Woman about carnal love, and that was the end of the Sun's perfect spiritual love. They were no longer misty-eyed. There was much less communing."

"So there was no forbidden fruit?"

"There might have been — it was a long time ago. So you see, I am father to the human race. I have always felt proud of that. I was father to Seth, the world's first Magician. I taught him a few things I wager your precious Magician friend does not know."

"But the semen you used was that of the First Man, so you are not really the father." The Fool paused momentously. "Whose semen are you using at the moment?"

"Not telling."

"You are loathsome! Whose semen is it?"

"I do not recall ... it is all mixed up."

That drew a line under the Fool's dalliance with the Devil. It was pointless, she thought, to expect much from the Devil, and once again she had been foolish. But yes, they could still be friends.

# ❧ 9 ❧

# COSMOGONY

*Turtles and Elephants:*
*concerning the incorrigible complexity of Beginnings.*

t was a quiet day in the market and the Fool was in the middle of a discussion about how the world began.

"Everybody knows it's turtles and elephants," said the Cheese Seller.

The Shoemaker interrupted. The Shoemaker was a literate man. "I read there was a giant cow that licked an iceberg, and inside the iceberg was a giant, frozen he was, and ... "

"You can't begin with a cow and an iceberg and a giant," the Magician interrupted with a cross expression on his face.

"Why not?" asked the Fool.

"Because simple explanations are better than complex explanations."

"But why?" the Fool said. "I like complicated explanations."

"Because there is an infinite number of complex explanations requiring increasingly improbable initial conditions — giant cows and frozen giants, and elephants standing on turtles for example. Simple explanations are more probable, because they do not require so many inexplicable things to be true simultaneously."

"You extinguish all imagination!" said the Fool, turning back to the Shoemaker. "Tell us about the frozen giant." So the Shoemaker told them about the giant and the tree and the squirrel that ran up and down the tree carrying gossip.

The discussion niggled at the Fool, and she decided she ought to consult someone reputed to know all the answers about how the world was made. She went to see the Hierophant. He resided in a sumptuous palace across the square from the Great Temple, and would sometimes appear on a balcony to lead prayers and blessings on high feast days. She was turned-away and stalled and misdirected by an interminable succession of clerks and secretaries and ecclesiastical busy-bodies. A mention of the Empress provided the necessary impetus to propel her through the barriers to access. "How is it," she thought, "that the Devil is so accessible and easy to talk to?"

"Well Child, what is it you need to know?" said the Hierophant, *Vicarius Solis* and Apostle of the Solar Logos.

"Father, I want to know how the world began. I have heard many conflicting stories."

"I can tell you traditions preserved from time immemorial by the Holy Temple of the Sun. Traditions that are widely promulgated by our ordained clergy, who would, if requested, provide you with instruction and insight."

"Is that not why I am here Father?"

"Um ... yes, I suppose so. You desire to know the story of Origins as told in the *Book of Beginnings*?"

"Yes! What came first? Was it turtles or elephants?"

"Ah ... the common folk, they are so resistant to instruction. I must always begin by refuting some wild fantasy that had its birth in taverns and idle chatter. This is the tradition: in the beginning there was some-

V The Hierophant

©C.A.L. 2017

thing I cannot describe to you, a glorious divine being beyond conception or description, limitless and eternal."

The Fool furrowed her brow and said, "Forgive me Father, I do not understand. Why would one introduce something beyond description? If it is beyond description then it is inaccessible to comprehension and all explanation is wasted … your Holiness?"

"A good point, indeed, an excellent point. However, St. Heliaustus argued that pure divine being beyond conception *is a logical necessity*. By definition one cannot speculate beyond the Beginning. You must see that? The Beginning is an epistemological boundary; one cannot, even in principle, have knowledge beyond the Beginning?"

The Fool nodded.

"And so *the least deficit of explanation* comes from a state of primordial simplicity. This simplicity, being without attributes, is beyond conception or description. A brilliant insight! It is a profound argument, divinely inspired beyond doubt. This thesis was endorsed by a Grand Synod of no less than three hundred bishops that took place in the reign of the Emperor Theophrastus II. We must consider pure divine being without attributes or description as beyond dispute … and insofar as we are unable to conceive of it, we must attribute this to our fallen condition." He smiled in a self-satisfied manner. "Let me continue … within this pure divine being, beyond conception or description, limitless and eternal, an empty space came into being." The *Vicarius Solis* paused dramatically.

"If divine being is limitless and eternal, is that not a contradiction Father?"

The Hierophant looked as if he was warming to the subject. "You ask how, if divine being is limitless and eternal, there can be both a unique moment of time, and a space empty of divine being? An excellent point, long debated. There is a bookcase in my library devoted solely to this question. Many say, and it is my own opinion, that these mysteries of the Beginning are not for us and it is sacrilege to speculate. It is our arrogance that demands explanations, like young children in a market who demand this or that, and howl and drag their feet and roll on the ground when they do not receive it. Explanations are a human weakness. The divine is beyond explanation; everything that we require to know has been given to us in the Sacred Books. We should marvel at their divinely-inspired wisdom and beauty."

"But the Sacred Books are withheld from us."

"For good reason, for good reason. A thousand lifetimes have been given to the interpretation and understanding of the Sacred Books. One must devote decades to their wisdom, and still one learns but a small part of all that has been written. And so we keep them from the frivolous and the foolish, for there lies the possibility of great harm. To give you but one example: according to the heretic Thomas of Cantabria the beginning is not a beginning. It both *is* and *is not*. There *is* empty space, but there is *no* empty space. Rather than doubt the lack of meaning in his assertions, he chose to doubt the validity of logic. This led to the appalling madness of the Thomasian heresy and so he was burned, but this gobbledegook still has adherents, and one of our leading contemporary theologians, Pascal Peres of Dondero, has argued — and I fear for his sanity — for a rehabilitation of Thomas."

"But Thomas is dead your Holiness."

"Only in the flesh my child. Only in the flesh. Now let us return to the space that appeared in the divine being. Many scholars assert that God 'made' the space through an act of divine will, but we must not view the verb 'made' too literally. This movement within God, a movement from passivity to activity, cannot be viewed in human terms. Doctrinally we say that it is a divine mystery revealed only to the Elect."

"And who are the Elect?"

"The Elect are those who are graced with divine revelation and insight."

"Are you one of the Elect Father?"

77

"This is a matter of individual grace and by tradition we do not speak of it. Let me continue. One can imagine an empty space of pure darkness, devoid of God, and a ray of divine light entered into it, so that there was light *and* darkness. And it is written that 'the darkness comprehended it not'. It is also written 'I formed light, and I created darkness'."

"What does that mean?"

"That God had to exclude himself to begin the creation, that space and darkness are not a part of God, and had to be created. Only the smallest part of God's light could enter this space or it would revert back to God again. Space and darkness are like a negation of God."

"Like the Devil?"

"In a manner of speaking. God is free, but space and darkness are fixed and definite, and all that is fixed and definite is bound by divine law and divine justice."

"Like when you make up a game, and everyone has to follow your rules, and you get to thump people if they don't behave?"

"I suppose so," said the Hierophant with a faint hint of weariness.

"What happened then your Holiness?"

"The light-in-darkness took the shape of a giant in the form of a human being. This was the Primordial Man, a being of pure radiant light, male and female combined in one. A glorious being."

"If you don't mind my impertinence in asking your Holiness, why do you call this being 'Primordial Man' if it is male and female combined? The High Priestess calls her 'The Great Mother' — which makes more sense if you ask me. She says that men are born of women and are formed from the flesh of women, and so are subsidiary beings, and it is for this reason that men have nipples, despite not suckling infants."

"In my opinion the High Priestess should guard her tongue and reacquaint herself with the sacred doctrine of the Holy Temple of the Sun," the Hierophant huffed. "The Primordial Man contains the

Divine Father and the Divine Mother who are ever conjoined in eternal love, and from that love they bear two children."

"The Sun and Moon?" suggested the Fool, finding solid ground.

"The Sun and Moon."

"Can I ask a question I have never understood. You speak of God and then you speak of the Sun, and yet we are taught that the Sun is God and the Sun is the creator who made the world and created human beings."

"Indeed, indeed, a simple matter. There is but one God, and the Sun is the outward sign of God. The Sun is God revealed to us. The creative power of God must reveal itself through eternal forms that give rise to the dynamic of the world, and so when we say that the Sun and Moon are children, we mean that the creative power has been reified and revealed. The Primordial Man is that full but hidden aspect of God that is revealed to us as the Sun."

"And if the Sun and the Moon were equal, why do we worship the Sun as God and not the Moon?"

"Ah ... in the beginning the Sun and Moon were born equally bright, but they quarrelled over whom should take first place. The Sun argued that there cannot be two rulers in the sky, just as there cannot be two rulers on one throne, for there lies the road to chaos. The Sun also argued that, just as courtiers bow their heads in the presence of a ruler, so the Moon and stars should avert their gaze and be humble while the Sun is in the sky. The Sun and Moon put their case to the Primordial Man, and the Moon lost, and she was diminished so that she had no light of her own, and what light she had was given to the Star to spread among all the stars."

"That seems so unfair!"

"But there could not be two Suns in the sky."

"So why did the Sun not lose his light. Why is it always the woman who has to be meek and dim and hidden?"

"That is the tradition. The Sun rules the day, the Moon and stars rule the night. So it is not unfair."

The Fool scowled grudgingly. The Hierophant continued.

"In the beginning I said that there was light, and there was a darkness that was space. The first creates, and gives life; the second encloses and binds a finite shape to all things, finite in space and finite in time. Life and death, good and evil, these are the founding principles of all that is. The Light is creative and gives, and the Space is limiting, and receives. And so there is in every aspect of existence a giving and a receiving. The Sun only gives, and so there is a shadow of the Sun that only takes."

"The Devil?"

"Indeed."

"And the Moon only takes, for she has no light of her own, and so there is an aspect of the Moon that only gives."

"The Star?"

"Indeed. I can see that you are not the Fool that your cap might indicate."

"Oh, I make terrible choices ... but I am not witless, if that is what you mean."

"Forgive me, I was being patronising."

"Is that not the essence of your role? I call you 'Father', you call me 'Child'. No need to apologise your Holiness." The Fool thought the Hierophant might have come close to blushing.

"Let me see, where were we?"

"One became two, who are forever joined, and two became another two who quarrelled and became four. I talked to the Devil and he said he was the Sun's brother."

"You talked to the Devil? I do hope you are not calling him up with forbidden black magic? Signing pacts? We don't approve of that."

"I just go round to see him and we converse. It is all straightforward and legitimate. I would not know where to begin with black magic."

"I am most relieved to hear that. So, technically, the Devil is not really the Sun's brother, more in the nature of a shadow. He does like to puff himself up. Father of Lies, never forget!"

"Have you met him your Holiness?"

"Goodness no! That would never do!"

"I thought the Sun and Moon were like opposites, but now I see that it is not so. There are four, not two."

"Indeed. Let me continue, for our time is limited. The Sun created the World and placed four great Watchtowers at the four quarters to mark the bounds of all-that-is ... and a great dome of stars to watch over us. He assigned four great spirits to guard the quarters — these are Harmozel, Oroiael, Davithe, and Eleleth. You will have seen them depicted as an Angel, a Bull, a Lion, and an Eagle."

"So why are there four Watchtowers and four great spirits?"

"They sustain the shape and character of existence. Were any to fail, then that aspect of existence would revert back to formlessness and chaos."

"Is the Devil chaos?"

"Fra. Pascal Peres, to whom I referred, asserts that evil is but an absence of good, and as a negation, evil has no being or substance. Some of the younger clergy are claiming there is no Devil. I cannot agree. St. Alonzo of Colona argues that there is a active power of despite and hatred that mocks all that is good, and that the Devil is bound to this world and walks among us. That the Devil hates the Sun and desires an end to all that is fine and beautiful."

"And will the Devil succeed?"

"There must be a great cleansing and purging before the perfection of the world is accomplished. The Devil and his minions must be routed and confined. According to the *Book of the Disclosing of the Culmination of Days* the Devil and all evil-doers will be bound in chains in a lake of fire. On that day all of existence will then be perfected, and the four Towers will come together and merge to become one great Holy City, and it will descend from the sky in glory like a bride robed for her wedding day. An angel will awaken the living and the dead, and all will rejoice and be free."

"And then what?"

"There will be a new world, a better world, a world without Death, and without the Devil."

"But is that not impossible your Holiness? You cannot have anything without its opposite ... you said so."

"Not in so many words, my child. And now I must go, for our time is complete."

And so the Hierophant went off to do something that involved choirs and a lot of incense.

What did he say?" asked the Cheese Seller. "Is it turtles and elephants?"

"It is turtles and elephants," the Fool replied, "all the way down."

# ❧10❧

# MEETING THE COINS

*In which the Fool encounters the source of all evil.*
*It is not the Devil.*

he Fool liked to idle in the Great Square on market days. There was a fruit stall whose owner would let her juggle with apples and pears, and sometimes he would let her keep one. She would caper and wisecrack and dance around for any stall holder who thought a small crowd would lead to more sales.

She was eating a hot pie and dribbling gravy down her chin when a hubbub of boos and hisses could be heard from where the lane from the North Gate joined the Square. A magnificent man on a horse entered the Square flanked by an escort of dangerous-looking thugs, and followed by a cart on which was seated an even more dangerous-looking ruffian quaffing ale from a wooden tankard.

"Who is that?" the Fool asked the Baker.

"The Prince of Coins, damn his eyes, come to collect our taxes."

"He looks so magnificent."

"He should do. We pays for his poxy magnificence. The Coins are a

83

bunch of blood-sucking leeches, the whole damned lot of them."

The boos and hisses grew as the procession crossed the square. Vegetables were thrown and people punched in the face, and a riot looked likely until city constables set about cracking heads and calming things down.

"Bloody Swords!" yelled the Baker, (he was referring to the constables), and turning to the Fool added, "The Coins pay 'em well — Coins takes our money, Swords beat us if we object. Parasites and rogues the lot o' them."

But the Fool was no longer paying attention. She had fallen madly in love with the glorious Prince in his fine clothes, riding the most noble horse she had seen. As if compelled by a mysterious force she followed the procession of Coins at a distance.

The Prince and cart left the city and travelled many miles before camping at a ruined farmstead she knew well. She joined the group, pretending to be going their way, and she entertained them with lewd jokes. She knew she was being foolish. The Prince's men looked like cut-throats and villains, but there was a large chest of money in the wagon and so she hoped they were less desperate than they appeared.

Her infatuation with the Prince knew no bounds. She flirted shamelessly, and in turn he was amused and attentive, for she greatly eased the tedium of the journey, and she was pretty and quick-witted.

"And have you always been a Fool?"

"Always my Lord. My mother said foolishness was in my blood, and that I would always be a flibbertigibbet and ne'er-do-well, with a mind as fixed as a grasshopper and restless as the wind."

"And do you not aspire to other things?"

"My Lord, it is said that aspiration is founded in discontent, and as I have no aspiration beyond the needs of the moment, I deduce that I must be happy."

"Then you are fortunate. You should meet my sister."

PRINCE OF COINS

"You have a sister my Lord?"

"Indeed. She aspires to greatness and is ever discontented."

"In what manner does she aspire to greatness?"

"She commissions great works in the modern style. Architects, painters and sculptors, she keeps them all busy with grand schemes and Father's money. Everything is torn down and remade. We live in eternal dust and hammering."

I must see these new things, the Fool thought. The Fool had an overwhelming fascination with novelty. She thought herself immune to discontent, but nothing dulled her spirit more than sameness and drudgery.

"Please Lord, may I see these things?"

"You shall. You shall meet my Sister, and my Mother and Father."

The group made its way through town and village, and everywhere they were cursed and reviled, though not to their faces.

"Yer should 'ave more sense than 'ang around with them blood-suckin' Coins," a washerwoman said. "Them's not good people."

"But I'm a Fool."

"Indeed you are dearie, indeed you are. What money have thee?"

"None."

"Then ye have no value. The glint o' gold is all they respect."

That hurt. The Fool, being foolish, thought nothing of dowries and inheritance, and assumed that love, good humour, and quick wit conquered all. "The Prince of Coins loves me. We are going to meet his family."

"Then he is a bigger fool than you are! Nothing like an old fool dearie."

"He is not old!"

In the fullness of time the wagon was so weighted with coin that its axles were groaning and shrieking and the driver was greasing them every mile. The hired villains grew ever more watchful. They were a vile bunch — lewd, cruel, and violent — but they were efficient with their fists and swords. Their leader was a southerner called Giuseppe. Despite a brutal appearance he was amiable and diligent, and the Fool sat with him on the bench seat of the cart.

"Why do you not just take the coin," she asked him.

"The King of Coins would put a bounty on our heads and none of us would live out a month. The pay is good and regular, the work is safe and satisfying, and there are rewards for service — promises of property, a place to retire to. A man could do worse."

The Fool learned more than she wanted to know about the mechanics of taxation. There were taxes and tolls and duties and tithes whenever goods were moved, or sold, or even looked at. The small folk gave their chickens and pigs and corn to the abbeys and to the local gentry, and it was stored in great barns. The cities enforced a myriad of duties on commerce, and every gate and bridge and half-made dirt track had someone claiming a hereditary right to charge a toll. Some part of everything was converted into coin and found its way into the great chest on the cart. It was all for the Emperor.

"But what does he do with it?" asked the Fool.

"The Emperor does not do anything with it," replied the Prince. "My father is Chancellor for the Emperor. *He* decides what to spend and where to spend it. Roads, bridges, harbours, abbeys, and of course, he has to pay the Swords."

"But the roads are terrible! The abbeys collect their own tithes. We pay tolls on all the bridges. The King of Swords has a feudal obligation to provide armed men in return for his land. Where is all this money going? What do the common folk receive in return for their bounty?"

"Peace and stability."

"But we are constantly at war."

"Wars are expensive. And castles and garrisons and watchtowers."

"But there are as many castles in the interior of the Empire as there are along our borders."

"There are many enemies within the Empire. Illyrian spies."

"You mean poor people?"

"Foreign powers are always attempting to cause dissension among the rabble."

The Fool sensed that this was not a good topic for conversation and resolved to ask the Hermit about it. He would know.

The journey ended and they approached an extraordinary estate. The Fool had seen many types of building, and they were, for the most part, utilitarian: shacks, byres, houses, halls, keeps, barns, guild-halls and so on. Decoration, where used, did not intrude on the primary purpose of the building. The buildings on the Coin estate were not like that. The primary purpose of walls was to support decoration. As there were insufficient walls, small buildings dotted the estate for no reason at all.

"Let me guess," said the Fool, "these must be follies. You knew I was coming."

"When my Sister has a passion there is no end to it," the Prince said wearily.

The main house — if it could be called that, for it could have housed a small town — was said to have over two hundred rooms. Most of them were filled with scaffolding and tradespeople of various kinds: plasterers, artists, sculptors, woodcarvers, gilders, glaziers, curtain hangers, carpenters, tilers, with countless apprentices rushing around on errands.

"You must meet my Sister. I cannot say where to find her, she could be anywhere."

The Queen of Coins was in her day room, a sanctuary from the chaos. She was inspecting a casket of jewellery.

"Mother, can I please introduce you to the Fool."

"A Fool ... how novel. Are we in preparation for a feast day? Will

QUEEN OF COINS

©G.A.S. 2017

there be entertainments? Delighted I am sure. Speaking of fools, your father called in a loan made to the Martellos. I expect you will recall them, their tithe barn caught fire and they lost their winter provisions. They borrowed money from us and were foolish enough to pledge their family jewels as surety. They defaulted, and here I have the entirety of their wealth!"

"I see an expression of delight on your face, Mother?" said the Prince.

"Much of this jewellery is not worth more than its weight in metal. But ... this solar disk on a chain is said to have belonged to St. Felix."

"The Cups will pay gold for that."

"I am arranging for one of your Father's scribes to produce a provenance. I think we have some old parchment somewhere."

"We have sufficient tradespeople on the estate to produce anything. We could produce a cathedral in an afternoon. We could pave the countryside as far as Illyria. A provenance will be child's play. Inform me if you require some confabulation of history to accompany this priceless and long-lost relic."

"We can talk about it later over wine. When you see your Father tell him we must take more care with jewellery as surety. People become sentimental about heirlooms and value them more than they are worth. We cannot afford sentiment, it is bad for business."

The Prince turned to the Fool. "My mother knows the value of everything, you know. Point to anything and she will tell you what it is worth. Never wrong."

"Extraordinary!" said the Fool. "I never know the value of anything."

The Queen regarded the Fool with a scornful expression.

"Let us go and meet Father," said the Prince.

The King of Coins was seated at the end of a large hall filled with clerks. There were ten rows of clerks, and each row had nine under-clerks, and, at the end of the row, an over-clerk standing at a slightly larger lectern.

"Foreclose on the Castellucios," the King shouted, pointing at an over-clerk. "What are their assets?"

"Three farmsteads Sire, good land."

"Growing what?"

"Sire, according to their last taxation, predominantly wheat, some livestock."

"The granaries are full again, there was ample wheat in the last harvest. Flax is the new thing. Evict the tenants."

"They have farmed the property as tenants for four generations Sire."

"They are old fashioned and failing to attend to the market."

"They have leases Sire."

"Worthless paper. Evict them, and pay Swords to attend our bail-iffs. Let them make a complaint in the courts if they can afford it."

"Of course Sire."

The Prince turned to the Fool. "Father does not reward ineffi-ciency. It is bad for the realm. There is a growing market for fine linen. With some reorganisation the farms will be worth more than the loan and we can auction them. We may even buy the properties ourselves."

"But what about the tenants?"

"Poor farming means low taxes. Farmers have a responsibility to the Empire, as do the rest of us. Father, I would like to introduce you to the Fool."

"Oh most excellent! I have long maintained that the growing wealth of the mercantile class will lead to a demand for entertainment. We must converse, I am sure it will be beneficial. Do make yourself at home. I cannot remain, I have to meet with a charming fellow called Ponzi. He claims to have an excellent new stratagem for making money."

"I met him Father. He is an unmitigated knave."

KING OF COINS

©C.A.L. 2017

"But they all are. It is a matter of discerning which rogues are most likely to make money. Then I find a way to become a partner in the bounty. If you understand my meaning."

"Yes Father."

The Prince led the Fool away. "I met that Ponzi fellow last month. He was going around the guilds looking for investors in a crooked scheme paying an implausible return. He asked me to vouch for him. I did not — he is a blackguard of course."

"So why do you not arrest him?"

"Father will squeeze him hard, you can be sure of that. But arrest him? What is the point? He will only cheat the gullible, and the fewer gullible folk we have, the stronger the realm will be. Ponzi is no more than a tax on stupidity, and we have a glut of that. Let us find my Sister."

They found the Princess staring at a ceiling writhing with gilded plaster decoration: acanthus leaves, putti blowing horns and carrying wreathes and banners, depictions of gods and goddesses, the Sun, more wreathes, more acanthus, heraldic shields and devices.

"I am so vexed!" she exclaimed. "The gilders are asking for more gold leaf ... again. You know how they dissemble, do you not? Thieves, the entire mendacious, scoundrelly bunch of them. I am sore tempted to hang them all."

"But then we would have a deficit of gilders," said the Prince, "and our many halls and chambers would be naked and unfinished. I can recommend what I do — cut the fingers off one of them, and that will inspire the rest."

"Then the Prince of Staves will come sniffing around. Do you know what he wants? It is an outrage! He wants craftspeople to form free associations to negotiate rates of pay."

"Like guilds?" asked the Prince.

"No, not at all like guilds. He asserts that the guilds are run for the

benefit of the Masters, and the Masters are toadys and brown-nosers
and snobs who aspire to join our class and who do not care about their
apprentices and journeymen."

"Impudence! We will not be sending him a Solstice card. Sister, I
would like to introduce you to the Fool."

"Oh, you are just delightful! I know we will be the very best of
friends! Come, let us find you something else to wear, you cannot wear
these clothes, people will think you a Fool."

"But I am a Fool."

"Oh, do not be preposterous, you have me laughing already. Your
apparel is most ironic — you have been to a festivity or a masque or
something highly fashionable. Let me ponder on't ... ah, I have the very
thing. It is an ensemble I wore last season, but do not concern yourself,
people here have no concept of fashion. Mother is still in the garb of
the last Emperor's court. They will think you are chic." The Princess
waved at the decor. "Do you not adore this, it is so modern."

"It is most intricate," observed the Fool.

"I am infinitely weary of classical, with all of the pretentious
formality and pomposity — porticoes, and columns, and architraves,
and pediments, and friezes. It is all so numbing and predictable and
joyless. I will die if I have to look at another gable above an entabla-
ture supported on columns and a tympanum in high relief showing
the divine order of the Sun and Planets. It is so overdone. The Cups
are so in love with harmony and proportion and divine reason. I want
romance, and nature and legend."

"There is plenty of Nature outside," the Fool observed, perhaps
more bluntly than she had intended.

"But it is so untidy and not very splendid. It all inclines to mud.
Nature has to be tended and tamed, its beauty won in a yearly struggle
with wind and winter. Gold is eternal. I would gild the lily. Come, let
us dress you up. Have you no other apparel with you?"

"Alas, the tribulations of travel. Your brother adopts a utilitarian

PRINCESS OF COINS

©C.A.L. 2017

mode of transport."

"Men, they lack sensitivity and refinement."

"Just so."

The Fool was guided to an overwhelming suite of rooms that (for all she knew) could have been the easterly annex of the West wing, or the westerly annex of the East wing. She was bathed in a large copper bath filled with rose-scented water. Maids trimmed and dressed her hair in the fashionable mode for an interminable time, while servants brought wine and sweets and fruit and other delicacies. Shoes with gilded buckles were found, and stockings, and underclothes, and sufficient ribbons to rig a schooner and moor her in a storm, or lash the entire crew to the masts, lest sirens entice them to their deaths. Her Foolish garb was removed for cleaning, and only her cap remained, shut away in a gilded cabinet. Her face was made, and a mirror brought.

"Why, I am quite adapted," she thought. "I must now be haughty and supercilious and condescending and overweening and pretentious, as fashion demands — such fine and ostentatious words, and it is a pleasure to have them support me in this charade. I am become the very handmaid of Folly, and I should revel in this excess. Fortune may not smile at me again."

There was an evening reception in a large salon filled with the cream of local society: merchants, guild masters, captains of mercenary companies, a few scholars in robes and black caps, and the extended family of the Coins. The Prince greeted the Fool with a great flourish, and she curtsied in reply.

"You have all the courtly graces. I knew you to be a Princess in disguise. How may I address you?"

"As I must remain unknown you should introduce me as the Princess Bianca, from a remote principality in the South. My father was Prince, but his brother plotted against him, and so we wandered abroad as common folk for reasons of safety. This is indeed a fair gathering."

"Much business is conducted in the form of light conversation and entertainment. We will eat, and then we will dance. Perhaps you will join me in the dance?"

"I would be greatly flattered and much honoured."

"Come and I will introduce you."

"My dear!" screamed the Princess. "You are most ravishing! I have an eye for these things, do I not Brother?"

"Indeed you do. You have the greatest refinement of taste."

"I am going to take you to Mother," said the Princess.

"Bianca," said the Prince over his shoulder. "Princess Bianca ... from the South."

"Mother, I would like you to meet ... Princess Bianca. From the South."

"Bianca, eh. From the South? So many principalities, I never could keep account of them. Some of them are no more than overgrown rocks with a few goats scampering about. But it is the blood that counts, is that not so girl?"

"Yes your Majesty," said the Princess Bianca. "The blood of the old families goes back to the first Empire, when the Sun ruled from a golden throne."

The Queen wagged her finger at the Princess of Coins. "Do you hear that Daughter? Blood! Tradition! That is why we should keep the *nouveau riche* at arm's length."

"And so we do Mother, so we do, at arm's length. But we should admit some merchants to our salons, for then our influence prospers."

"I find this mercantile class distasteful. Their fathers were peasants. So Bianca, what does your family possess besides blood and a long memory for ancestors?"

"Alas, my father was betrayed by his brother, and was cast out from his rightful estate."

"A common story in these times. I expect your dowry is locked in your uncle's storeroom?"

"My dowry is much diminished, and I am reduced to my wits."

"And your beauty it would seem."

"Thank you your Majesty. You are most gracious."

"Tell me ... Princess Bianca, what is the future of wealth? Some say land is the foundation of wealth. Some say trade. Some say manufacture. I am inclined towards the permanence of gold. What is your opinion on the future of wealth."

"In the future," said the Princess Bianca, "wealth will lie in paper."

"You mean books? How so?" asked the Queen.

"Not books your Majesty. With your permission, I have a question for the Princess." The Princess Bianca turned towards the Princess of Coins. "When you commission an artisan, your steward issues a paper describing the work and the future payment. When the work is completed the artisan returns to the steward and is paid the sum on the paper. Is this not so?"

"As you say."

"The chests of guild masters are stuffed with these papers. Their work is complete, but they wait for payment. Payment is often delayed, sometimes for months, sometimes for years. Apprentices need to be fed, and tools and materials bought, and so masters trade your paper. You promise to pay one hundred silver coins in two Moons, but a master in straits will take eighty-five coins today rather than wait out the delay."

"You say that our promises have value?" asked the Queen.

"Trust has value," said the Princess Bianca. "You have only to put your seal to paper and it is as good as metal. And there is a shortage of metal. The business of collecting taxes is burdened by the weight of copper coin, for there is insufficient silver and gold for the current fury of commerce and trade. Your carts are destroyed by the weight of copper."

"So we keep the gold in the cellar, and yet we still own the paper. The paper we hand out comes back to us, and so we hand it out again. What a merry game you have devised!"

"It is not of my devising. It was invented in the East, where gold is scarce, and the weight of metal grew too cumbersome for trade. The metal rests behind walls, and its trade is accounted in tokens."

They talked, and the Fool was delighted with her new friends, for they were quick and perceptive and she loved to match her wits. Later she danced, and forgot she was a Fool.

Sitting up in bed, waiting for his wife to complete her evening toilet, the King of Coins said: "This Princess Bianca ... what say you?"

"Quick as a whip, educated, claims to hail from the South, but her speech lacks the uncouth diction of those parts. Comfortable with the manners of court, and dances with the grace of familiarity ... and dance is a sure sign of breeding. Her guise as a travelling Fool is an eccentricity beyond any reasonable reckoning. What say you?"

"Not a penny to her name, but pretty, and we should grant the boy some credit for good taste. An agreeable companion. But he always had a predilection for strays."

"Yes, we have had our fill of mangy kittens and puppies creeping underfoot. There will be tears I think."

There were to be no tears — at least, not for the Fool. After some weeks of delightful excess the Princess Bianca had quite forgotten her Fool's cap in the gilded cupboard, and enjoyed a life of luxury in the company of the Princess of Coins. They planned new follies together, larger and more ornate. They were swarmed about by seamstresses imported from the most fashionable courts. She danced and slept with the Prince, and enjoyed long and spirited discussions with the King on the quantification of risk and the discounting of promissory notes.

"She is the most remarkable companion," said the King. "I am inclined towards a new belief that a dowry of wits and beauty may be no small thing."

"You would think that," said the Queen. "Nothing more than a pretty face and an agreeable smile would suffice for your taste. I think a dowry of gold would add everything to her prospects. I have sent agents to the South."

One night the Fool awoke to find the Devil sitting at the foot of her bed.

"You must not be here! I may be burned!"

"I approve of your new companions, but I miss your company."

"Go, go! ... In what manner approve?"

"Devoted to gain. They desire the whole pie. Nothing stands in their path. They would throw a baby into a mire that their passage be less impeded. I applaud them."

"They are charming and kind, and treat me with affection and courtesy."

"And will you throw the baby into the mire when they request it?"

"You are more foolish than I. Now go lest I ... lest I ... just go!"

"When will I see you?"

"I am busy and content, now go!"

The Devil went, but Devils have a tradition of spoiling happy situations with apples, pomegranates, figs, and other tokens of unsought illumination, and so it was that the Devil left his mark on the Fool's happy garden of delight. There was a worm in the apple, and now that she saw it, she could not unsee it. She sat for many hours, found her motley clothes and her jester's cap, gathered her few possessions into her satchel, and crept out of the gate past a sleeping watchman as dawn lit the eastern sky.

# ❧11❧

# THE WHEEL OF FORTUNE

*In which the Wheel of Fortune and its Master are removed through ill-fortune.
It is replaced by a mighty Wheel of Cosmic Destiny.
It also tells the time.*

For many years one of the more memorable features of the fairs held in the Great Square was a great and gaudy Wheel of Fortune run by a flamboyant character called Master Percival. He dressed like a wealthy burgher, and had long waxed moustachios styled in an outlandish fashion that was unique throughout the city. The Wheel was spun, bets were placed, and Master Percival would scowl ferociously whenever he had to pay out money on a bet.

There was always a crowd of idlers commenting on the play, debating strategies, cheering runs of good luck, and bemoaning episodes of ill-fortune. The single overriding urge that united all comers was a desire to best the wicked Master Percival, who seemed less than human and more the earthly right-hand of a perverse and inconsistent Providence.

"It's fixed I tell ye!"

"'Ow's it fixed then? There's nowt to it, it's just an wheel on an axle."

"It's weighted. There's lead sunk in the rim, you mark my words, there's sommat not right wi' it. Watch how often it stops on black."

Black paid out nothing.

"The constables check it every market day, and any time they feels like it too. Seen 'em do it, test the balance, see it dun't swing of its own accord. Think they would bet if it wus weighted?"

"He pays 'em off. Slips 'em silver, mark my words."

"What's the point in cheatin' if he has to pay off the constables. You know what they are like, bunch o' vermin, bleed 'im dry like as not."

"Sommat's not right!"

"Go and check for yourself. Plenty does. He dun't mind."

"The way he scowls — he has summat to hide. There's no good in that man."

"Its just theatre. The crowd loves it when he loses."

The Fool had listened to the arguments. She had spent countless hours cheering and groaning as rich and poor tried their luck against the merciless spin of the wheel. It was the best free show in the City. When she had a few coppers she would place a bet and time would stop as the massive wheel spun. When it had slowed to a crawl it would tease the punters, holding out the certainty of a win. And then, finding some last residue of momentum, it would crawl on past to the adjacent number. There would be howls and groans. The eyes of the crowd would move from the faces of the losers to that of Master Percival. Even as he swept his winnings off the table and into his pouch the Master Percival looked unhappy. When he lost, his scowls were like to curdle fresh milk.

The Cups argued that the Wheel deprived the poor of their hard-earned wages, and families went hungry because of it (which was true). They preached against the evils of gambling and the iniquities of Master Percival, whom they feared to refer to by name as he was clearly an emissary of the Devil.

The poor were capable of formulating a excellent reply to this critique (which they muttered in private, over tankards). It was that tithes and taxes also deprived them of wages, but without the element of entertainment or the possibility of providential riches. And taxation was a singularly unrewarding form of entertainment.

Master Percival died during a hot summer when the rivers ran dry and the bloody flux went through the City. The Fool had gone north into the mountains, and when she returned for the next market day she found the Wheel was no more. The opinion of the priests had prevailed on the city council. Some idlers had come forward claiming to have inherited the Wheel but a license was refused. In its place was something new and extraordinary.

"What is it?" she asked the Shoemaker, who liked to keep a finger on the pulse of modernity.

"It is a simulacrum. It embodies the rational order of the cosmos, and the transmission of celestial influences into the mundane sphere."

"I am amazed!" said the Fool, who was amazed. "This contrivance goes far beyond the whims of an erratic Fortune."

"As you will know, the mundane world is the reification of a higher order of being that is embodied in the imperfect matrix of substance."

"How came you by these insights?"

"'Tis the wisdom of Hermes, as outlined in the *Intelligible Order of the World*."

"Hermes? You are now become a scholar of Hermes?"

"I am much encouraged by the Magician. It is the logical step from Plautus. And it is the Magician who conceived this work — he designed it for the King of Cups."

The Fool went to see the Magician, who was completing a performance of sleight-of-hand by the fountain at the centre of the Square.

"That new thing over there. What is it?"

"It's a Clockke."

"A what?"

X THE WHEEL OF FORTUNE

"A Clockke. It shows you where the Sun is."

"But I know where the Sun is. I can see it."

"It shows where the Sun is ... more precisely."

"But I know where the Sun is ever so precisely. It's right behind that chimney over there."

"But what if it was cloudy. Or you were in a cave."

"But that Clockke thing is much too large to take into a cave. And why must I know where the Sun is if I am in a cave?"

"Well, at night then. You can tell where the Sun is at night."

"But I know where the Sun is at night. He is in his palace in the West. He has dinner. Then he sorts through prayers and petitions, just like any king. Then he goes to sleep."

"Well, if you could imagine that instead of doing these things the Sun continues to drive his chariot around the back of the world, it shows you where he would be if he was not in bed."

"What is the use of that? Everyone else is in bed too."

"Apart from Cups. They wake for Matins, the night prayers to guarantee the Sun's safe return."

"Ah yes, the clamour of bells every night."

"Indeed. The King of Cups would like a better system to tell priests when to wake in the night. Some temples take pride in being the most zealous and so first to ring Matins. Others insist on determining the time with utmost diligence using nothing more than sand timers and candles. There is no concordance, and so there is a cacophony of bells throughout the small hours. There have been deputations from bakers and the mothers of young babies and the like, suggesting they sort themselves out. And so the King of Cups asked me to design a mechanical Sun, with the option of making it ring bells as a complement to the *Liturgia Horarum*. 'That thing' as you put it, is a prototype. If it is popular I expect we will go into production. The smiths are keen on it — clockkes are excellent application for their skills. There is talk of using it for meetings."

"Meetings? Is it not that people simply turn up? The meeting begins when the most powerful person is ready. And anyone who is late is flogged or appointed to manage the daily collection of night soil?"

"There is a demand for more meetings. At the moment it is difficult to organise more than two or three meetings a day. With a mechanical Sun we could divide the day into regular intervals."

"But then everyone would need a mechanical Sun."

"I thought ... and I need to discuss this with the King ... that we could stick a clockke in the Temple tower and it could work some bells, say, ninety-six times a day."

"People would hate that. Especially the bakers. And mothers of young babies."

"We could tell them that these bells drive away evil spirits."

"But, but ... this is no different from a priest with a sand timer ringing a bell ninety-six times a day and driving everyone to madness."

"Ah, but that would require three priests working in succession, for one alone could not endure the tedium and discipline. I have made the calculation. This Clockke is more efficient and modern."

The Fool understood that once the Magician had said the word 'modern' that there was no further argument that one could make. 'Modern' trumped all further arguments. 'Modern' implied novelty, and novelty was intrinsically fascinating because it disclosed an aspect of existence previously hidden from sight. Modernity was a continuous revelation of mystery, like a scroll being unrolled.

"So that is all it does? Imitate the Sun? It looks more complicated."

"Oh, once I had comprehended the simulation of the Sun I understood that I could provide the Moon and Planets as well. And the stars. Everything in the heavens, bar the impenetrable darkness. I have yet to devise a means to predict the erratic appearance of comets signifying wars and pestilence and the death of princes. Nevertheless, you can see at a glance that Venus and Mars are conjunct, that the Moon is trine with Jupiter, and that Mercury is rising in Virgo."

"Most marvellous!" said the Fool doubtfully.

"Our bodies are microcosms that respond to the influences of the heavens. Temperament, good fortune, energy, sickness and health — these are all prefigured by patterns in the sky. The destiny of kings and empires are all there for those with the knowledge to read the aspects. The Sun sends warmth and light and growing power into the world. The Moon moves the sea, and tides within the bodies of women, and rules the creatures of the night. Mars is the virile power of energy and war and strife, Venus the power of love and marriage and beauty, Mercury the power of quickness and intelligence and knowledge of many things. Jupiter is good fortune and abundance and prosperity, but terrible with retribution if ill-aspected."

"And Saturn?"

"Old age. Death. The earth and all that is buried and concealed within it. Rebirth. Great ages of time."

"Extraordinary! And you can tell all of this from your Clockke?"

"Wonderful, is it not? A complete simulation of the Cosmos, demonstrating the rational and comprehensible basis of divine order. It is a glimpse into the mind of God."

"I must presume by this you intend the Sun?"

"There is another, greater God."

"How can that be so?"

"The Sun obeys the strictures of reason, and so there must be a mind that is greater than the Sun."

"Hush, you must not say that."

"But the Sun is merely a part of a greater scheme."

"Do you say that the Sun and Moon are children of the Primordial Man, as the Hierophant asserts?"

"I say that the Sun and Moon belong in the world of geometrical determination, and are reflections of a higher realm of number and proportion."

"You really must not say that, or they will burn you in the square next to your Clockke. You will be naught but a pile of ash, and the wind will take you and blow you about."

"Fie on that. First the Cups request a Clockke, then they would stop my mouth lest I o'erturn their theological apple-cart with the deductions they require I make *for their benefit?*"

"Shhh ... be not so heated. They must arrive at your opinion in time."

"I suppose there is that. The man who makes the Clockke wins the dispute."

# ❦12❧

# NOT MEETING THE SUN

*The Fool attempts to meet the Sun without an appointment.*
*The Moon has time to chat.*

he Fool loved the Sun. Nights on the road were cold, and she loved the slanting yellow warmth of dawn. She loved the sound of birds waking, preening themselves, chirping to discover their neighbours. She loved springtime, when the new leaves were most fresh and most green, and every green was new and fresh, and every green was different, a breathtaking palette of green. The Sun brought life, and a joyful thrill in all living things that sought warmth and light.

There were hot summer days when she tired of the heat and dust and flies, and the constant need to find good water, but she reflected that all love was mixed. One could have too much of a good thing. Sometimes she needed an absence from the heat, a little shade, a shower of rain, a warm night under a moonlit sky.

She resolved to thank the Sun in her own way. It was true that the Hierophant organised many kinds of communal thanksgiving ceremonies, but they were formal and rather dull:

"We give thanks to thee O Sun, for thy life-giving warmth that ripens the grain, and for our daily bread blah blah blah." This staid and stuffy thanksgiving was not the sort of thing a Fool could sit still for. She wanted to give thanks personally, face to face, and she wanted to see what the Sun was like close up.

The obvious and most immediate problem was that the Sun seemed to be a long way off, even from the top of the highest hills. She reasoned that the best way to meet the Sun would be in the morning when he was rising, or in the evening just before he went to bed.

But she recalled that she hated being imposed upon by random strangers in the morning when she was still grumpy and sleepy, and perhaps evening would be better. But then, he might be equally grumpy after shining all day, and there were the horses and chariot to take care of. You cannot drive horses all day and then shoo them off because you are tired, she thought. You need to look after them. It was well-known that the Sun used a *quadriga*, or chariot drawn by four golden horses, and the Fool had seen a gilded bronze likeness on the triumphal arch leading to the great Temple of the Sun. She hoped she might see the Sun's splendid horses. The Fool liked horses.

After much thought on the matter she chose to travel West. West is best, she thought, and liked that it rhymed. Easterly is beasterly, and westerly is besterly.

It took many days of walking to the West to reach the house of the Sun. There was a great hubbub, a bustle of noise and activity as the Muse Urania prepared the Moon and stars for their entry onto the celestial stage. Urania was watching a collection of sand timers on a table, each labelled with the name of a constellation.

"Taurus, are you ready? Aldebaran, can you organise the Hyades for me, they seem exceptionally addle-brained today. Orion! You go out after Taurus." She turned to the Fool.

"You would think they would know the order after so many aeons, but every night they are as empty-headed and disorganised as the night before! Gemini wants to go out with Aquarius. What are they thinking!"

"I thought they rose in the East?"

"Yes, of course they do, they pop around the back of the world. I know it must seem strange, but it is easier this way. I account for the stars as they set and report to me in the West, and so I am better able to organise the stars going out. You must trust me on this. I tried waiting around in the East and the stars would never turn up on time. Or at all. The mages of Stygia were exceedingly perplexed, having spent three centuries refining their calendrical calculations."

"So the Earth is not round?"

"Of course not! Whoever gave you that idea? How would the Sun rest?"

"My thoughts also. I would like to see the Sun."

"The Sun? He came in a few minutes ago. You should talk to Clio, she keeps the daily journal. It used to be Mnemosyne, but she retired."

The Sun's house was very grand, very classical, all columns and architraves and porticoes and friezes. There were several courtyards where Muses were instructing classes in the finer aspects of dance and poetry and drama. The one discordant element in this scene of elegance and proportion was a background shrieking of "It's ruined!" and "You've spoiled it!" and "It will never work!", interspersed with wails and howls of intense grief.

The Fool found Clio. "What is that discordant clamour?"

"It is Melpomene — she provides us with an insight into the nature of Tragedy. Please ignore it, you will become accustomed to it after a time. What may I do for you?"

"I desire to see the Sun."

"You cannot see the Sun tonight," said Clio. "People spend the day praying and petitioning and requesting that He should bless this and that, and it all accumulates. I keep the record of every prayer and petition, and first thing He does when He comes in is pick it up and He will be going through it now."

"So when can I see Him?"

"You are a Fool, are you not? Not very important?"

"I am wholly unimportant."

"Have you thought about talking to a priest? One of the Cups? That is how it works. We set up a system of priestly intercession for this reason. There is little purpose in having a priesthood if people think they can drop in for a personal interview. The Sun is the centre of the Cosmos and the source of all life. He has a lot to do."

"I am sorry, I did not think."

"I am pleased you understand. When I saw your cap with bells I guessed that forethought might not be your *forte*."

"The strength of my passions incline me to Folly. But I have a pleasing nature, and my company is sought by many. May I say that of all the Muses you are the most accomplished and renowned. I have heard your name spoken before any other."

"Why, thank you. I do not always feel recognised among so much talent. Now that I consider your situation, I recall that the Moon is not due to rise for an hour, and I could accommodate you with her. As you have come all this way, making this long journey to the West."

Now the Fool had often envied the High Priestess, with her seem-ingly easy access to the Moon, and it took her less than one second to conclude that this was a fair and decent offer.

"Yes please, I would love to see the Moon, perhaps I could see the Sun some other day?"

"Yes, perhaps. Come this way."

The Moon was at her dressing table checking her face. "Sit down dearie, sit down, I am two days short of full so I have to look my best. The stars don't like it when I outshine them, and they say vile things. They are a rabble of air-headed flibbertigibbets. Well, not all of

112

them — Sirius is a notable exception."

"You mean Sothis?"

"Sothis? Yes, Sothis, that is her name in the South. Some people call her the Dog Star because she is in Canis Major, but I think that unkind. Now Algol, there is a star with a changeable disposition. What may I do for you?"

"I wanted to converse if I may. I planned to tell the Sun how splendid He is, but it seems He is much occupied. But you are also magnificent. I always look out for you. When I am alone in the woods and on the hills, you are my company."

"Am I? How wonderful! I do my best. It is a struggle some days, fighting with the clouds for space in the sky, but I do my best with the little light I can borrow."

"I was told you were once as bright as the Sun, and you gave your light to the stars."

"I did, I did. I cannot recall what came over me, and there is not a day when I do not wonder why I bothered with those silly little pin-pricks of frivolity. But the Sun? I have no regrets, I could not do the Sun thing. He has to wear the same face every day. Me? I have a different face every day, and I enjoy that. Also He cannot witness the beauty of the night, or any of its creatures, whereas I am able to see both night and day. He is unable to see the patterns of the stars ... which is probably a blessing come to think of it. And He has so much work to do when He comes home in the evening: petitions, healing, miracles, prophetic dreams. Very few bother me now — a few witches, and of course, the mad. Are you mad my dear?"

"Mostly foolish. But many some have called me mad, and there may be substance to the claim."

"In that case we will be boon companions. Werewolves, the barking mad, the howling mad, mad dogs, night owls, night mares. Mares in general — that is a jest you know — ah, the sea, the sea, ebbing and flowing, tides and time. What is a day? Why, nothing! But a month —

that is real time."

A realisation crept over the Fool that the Moon might be two days short of full in more ways than one, and her long association with disordered wits might be one of affinity.

"Is it true that the Sun is your brother?"

"Brother, lover, what does it matter, we are spiritual beings you know. We are duals, heavenly jewels, partners in the grand minuet of time, light and dark, stepping out the days, months and years."

"But you were as bright as the Sun?"

"I was, but I gave it away, and now look at me, painting my face on while the Sun tells the Muses about a magnificent new heroic metre He has just devised. But I will have my light again when the stars fall from the sky, and then we will see who is brightest."

"I am sure you will be the brightest. And the most beautiful. And everyone will worship you, and not the silly old Sun."

"Hush, you must not say that. But thank you dear." The Moon stood up and adjusted her skirts. "I am ready. I hope you will excuse me but Urania will be around fussing if I fail to appear. She has all those silly timers you know, and there is one with my name on it."

"I expect there are sailors are waiting for the tide," said the Fool, "And fishes in the sea, and a secret world of life that moves to your rhythms, a tide of eggs waiting for a signal to enter the world. Shine bright O Moon!"

"Blessed be! I will, I will!"

The Moon left the room and the night sky grew bright. In the distance there was a howling as wolves sang their greeting. The Fool felt sad and yet strangely encouraged. "Perhaps I have also lost some of my light. But I will find it again, and shine as brightly as any Sun."

# ✣13✣

# MEETING DEATH

*In which the Fool attempts to enlist Death in her little schemes.*

he Fool had been camping on the floor of the Magician's basement. The talk in the City was of the General, the continuing warfare along the Illyrian border, and the effect on trade.

"I have heard enough of war," the Fool said to the Magician, "I want to meet with Death."

"Knives, poison, disease, runaway horses, that sort of thing?"

"I had in mind something more conversational."

"Ah, you want to talk to Death. But why?"

"The General. I want to be rid of him. I thought Death might like to assist."

"You want to summon Death to come and take the General? Is that not the very pith and essence of black magic?"

"Not necessarily summon — I am prepared to travel. And you are being melodramatic. I merely wanted to explore the many possibilities leading the General's eventual demise."

"With Death?"

"Yes."

"And you are prepared to travel?"

"Yes."

The Magician stared into space for a minute. "There was a great enchantress in the Golden Age and it is written that she knew how to summon Death. For the purpose of exploring possibilities, just as you say. I have a book somewhere. It was on this shelf right here. Right there! You can see the space!"

"How do you remember where everything is? This place has all the domesticity of a pigsty."

"I remember where everything was. This is infuriating! I am convinced someone goes around the room moving things just to make me insane. And I observe that I should not have guests, especially those with opinions on housekeeping. Ah, here it is supporting this beaker. Let me see ... let me see ... here we are. You must travel to the Ends of the Earth. Well, that is a farrago of nonsense to begin with. There is no end to the Earth. The world is like a ball, you keep going around and around like a dog chasing its tail."

"But I have been there."

"To the Ends of the Earth?"

"Yes."

"This would appear to be one of your wildly fantastic tavern stories. And water pours over the edge?"

"Where the Sun has his palace in the West. And there are Four Towers, one in each direction, at the Cardinal Points."

"Ah, that story, Four Towers that prevent the world from collapsing back into nothingness."

"So I must travel to the Ends of the Earth. This I can do. What then?"

"You will find a cave that is an entrance to the underworld, where Death rules over the land of the dead, and all is dust and ashes. You should dig a hole a cubit wide and a cubit deep using a sword, just outside the cave."

"A sword? And what of the current fashion for blades like skewers? All the bravos are strutting around with skewers at their belts. How is one to shift earth with a skewer? Can I not employ a mattock for the same purpose?"

"It does not say. These ancient instructions are inscrutable and insist on the strangest details. Then you must use the sword to cut the throats of sheep and let the blood drain into the hole — it would seem that the use of a sword is for reasons of economy, that the traveller not be overburdened, there is nothing that *prohibits* the use of a mattock."

"Where do these sheep come from?"

"From mummy sheep I would imagine."

"So I require a mattock and a sword and a herd of sheep. What further details are there?"

"You must stand guard over the blood in the hole. The spirits of the dead will rise up out of the cave, and you must prevent them from drinking the blood by using the sword."

"So I must engage in swordplay while beset by thirsty, hungry ghosts rising up in countless numbers from the realm of the dead. What then?"

"After a time the Queen of the Dead will come and drink some blood, and regain her memory of being human, for she once lived in this world. She will recover the power of speech and she will be able to talk with you."

"But I want to talk to Death. Not the Queen."

"That is all it says. Perhaps the Queen can tell you what you need to know."

"There has to be a better way. If this ancient author had any knowledge of the Ends of the Earth he would know it to be somewhat deficient in agriculture. And solid ground for that matter, and certainly sheep. If there is one thing one can be sure of at the End of the Earth, it is that the earth has ended.

"There is nothing in life more certain than tautology," observed the Magician.

"One might argue," continued the Fool, warming to the idea, "that there *could* be stray sheep clambering about the rocky skirts of the fathomless abyss, as sheep are wont to do. But if they *are* there, I lack the ability to pursue them. Besides, I like sheep. I am not killing sheep. There is little utility in Death if I have to kill the sheep."

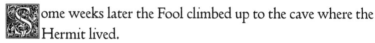ome weeks later the Fool climbed up to the cave where the Hermit lived.

"I want to meet with Death," said the Fool to the Hermit.

"He was around. He is always around. He likes to chat to Justice."

"Have you seen Death?" said the Fool to Justice.

"You have chosen an ill day. Death is much occupied. The General is punishing the Illyrians for violating a treaty they had to sign under duress."

"I do not understand."

"The General is burning villages and slaughtering farmers to teach them a lesson."

"That is deplorable. The General is slaughtering poor farmers, and yet Death attends to the farmers? You are Justice, why do you not do something? Would it not be less effort for Death to attend to the General? A misdirected arrow? A bolt of lightning? Surely the bloody flux is a common misfortune among soldiers?"

"I have to arrange everything with Necessity! Necessity!" Justice could sound shrill when pressed. "Necessity is utterly unbending in matters of protocol. If the thread of the General's life stretches on past this point, I have no power to change it. Even Death attends Necessity like a dog at the beck and call of its owner. Your temper is itself unjust and most unwelcome. I plead with you to amend it."

"I beg your forgiveness. Would you kindly call me when Death returns, for I would pursue this matter."

"I will summon you most promptly."

Justice summoned the Fool with a shout. The Fool had a short conversation with Death. There were no sheep involved.

"I don't do requests," said Death.

"Oh," said the Fool.

"He does not do requests," the Fool said to the Hermit.

"I did not think he would," said the Hermit.

The Fool met with the Magician some weeks later.

"I met with Death. He does not do requests, more is the pity."

"So the entire science of Black Magic is undone?" observed the Magician.

"Not the entire science," said the Fool. "The Devil might have some utility in this matter."

"There is that. But you said the Devil is idle and contrary, unlike Death, who is industrious and implacable."

"Yes, one can depend on Death. The good news is that I did not need the sheep. Or the mattock. Or the sword."

"It grieves me to have purchased so many ancient authors at vast expense," said the Magician, indicating his bookcases, "only to have their testimony undermined by the confabulations of a Fool."

"In that case, perhaps you could write a new book," said the Fool. "At vast expense. With me in it."

# Playing the Fool

# 14

# MEETING THE CUPS

*In which we encounter a desire for the Ideal and the Miraculous.*

ach year for the three days around the first Sunday after the Summer Solstice there was a great fair in the City. The fair was a celebration of *Sol Invictus*, the invincible and unconquerable Sun in his full majesty and glory. The festival was a formal occasion, unlike the drunken and riotous winter solstice holiday. By tradition the Prince of Cups gave a noon sermon in the Temple. The highlight of the festival was the moment when the Queen of Cups drew down the healing light of the Sun and blessed the water from the fountain in the Great Square. Thousands travelled from the countryside to drink the waters.

There were no rooms to be had for any reasonable sum of money, and the Fool was offered a place on the floor of the Magician's cluttered apartment. They went to the Temple together with other market regulars — the Shoemaker, the Baker, the Potter, the Fishwife, and sundry other idlers who liked to chatter.

The Temple was filled with Cups, who had travelled from temples, abbeys, and monasteries in their grandest robes of office (or humblest habits of penitence, according to status and temperament) to hear their Prince. They carried banners, solar monstrances and reliquaries, golden sun-disks on poles, and golden statues of the Sun according to the approved iconography: a beautiful athletic man in his prime with a corona of golden rays surrounding his head.

The Prince entered the *pulpitum* high above the common folk and gave the traditional sermon: that they should all aspire to be like unto the Sun, who shines on all equally. But light creates shadow. Those who live in the Sun's glorious light without themselves sharing that light create a shadow, and shadow is the essence of the Evil One, and of the Great Serpent that attempted (at irregular intervals) to swallow the Sun.

"There isn't really a serpent," the Magician muttered *sotto voce*, "It's the Moon."

The Baker's wife looked shocked, as did the Potter, who said "Shhhh...!"

"You must not say that," said the Fool. "Of course there is a Great Serpent. And it tempted the First Man and the First Woman, and it girds the entire cosmos and tries to eat our souls when we die."

"He gives the same sermon every year," said the Potter. "Always we should be like the Sun. Always. Every year."

"What else should we be like?" asked the Baker, "Turnips?"

"There are many young people newly attending," said the Fool, "and they will not have heard it before."

"His sermon is an elaboration of Werburgh's Golden Rule," observed the Shoemaker. "Love your neighbour as yourself, do unto others as you would have done unto you, be nice to others, classic St. Werburgh."

"What?" asked the Potter.

"St. Werburgh, *Mysterium Solis*, you should read it. The Golden Rule, being like unto the Sun. It is all in there. You can borrow my copy."

"Not enough time," replied the Potter. "And if I did 'ave the time, oi'd spend it doin' ter others as they do ter me."

"Eh?"

"Given 'em a smack in the kisser fer nickin' me pots and passin' bad coin."

There was a discussion on the prevalence of bad coin. It was a perennial topic. The Magician knew all of the tricks.

"Roll out copper between gold leaf and then stamp it like normal."

"Easy to tell," said the Baker, "You just bites it. And nobody passes gold fer bread in any case."

"You can do the same with silver. And you can stamp copper and then cover it with silver foil and fuse them together."

"Bastards!"

"And for gold, one can gild lead using gold dissolved in mercury. The weight feels right, and it's soft too — difficult to spot."

"Bastards!"

"It's the clippers as I can't stand," said the Potter. "One coin in three been clipped. An' folks still want me to take 'em. The poor widow 'as gone an' dropped and broke 'er only jug, and I take the clipped silver 'cos it is all she 'as an' she ain't got none other."

"It is said," said the Fishwife, "It is said, as Coins been mixin' copper in the silver at the Mint. At the Mint! That ain't right that ain't. Emp'rer needs be payin' attention. Can't be messin' wi' the coin. Got 'is head stamped on it, ter say it's proper coin an' all."

"It is true," said the Magician. "My friend Gharani the goldsmith complains of this. There is not enough silver in the realm to mint new coin, and what store we have is buried in the ground to keep it safe, or lost at sea, and yet more is melted down to make charms and badges and other pilgrim trinkets, so the shortfall is made up using copper. Another problem is an imbalance of trade — we imported grain after the wet summer three years ago, and we are not exporting enough to cover

KING OF CUPS

©C.A.L. 2017

the cost, so the Empire is losing silver."

"Time for another war," observed the Shoemaker, "we can go and fetch it back."

"Indeed," said the Magician. "That is about the only thing the Swords are good for — extracting silver from the houses of our neighbours."

"Bastards all of 'em," hissed the Baker. "And ... ," he continued, "and ... 'ow come the Cups be tellin' us to be kind an' all, to give generously to widows and the sick when they be so bleedin' rich theyselfs!!"

This was a perennial sore point. Everyone agreed the Cups were essentially decent, and they provided hospices and schools, and almshouses for the needy, and there was always a Cup who would come to bless a birth, or a marriage, or bury the dead, but no-one could ignore the stupefying wealth of the great abbeys and cathedrals and monasteries.

According to the prevailing orthodoxy the Sun had made another world, a realm of the blessed, and deserving worshippers would be selected to live there after death. It had become the custom to bestow fortunes and legacies on the Temple in the belief that this might improve the possibility of being chosen.

Another factor behind the burgeoning wealth of the Temple was the custom among Swords and Coins to leave property only to the eldest child as a way of preserving landholdings and family power. The younger siblings were left to make their own way in the world, and many saw the Temple as an ideal way to continue a life of luxury and ease. Once ensconced in the hierarchy of the Temple their instinct was not a life of humility and service for the common good. Their instinct was to devise elaborate marketing and money-making enterprises, and so temples and abbeys would trumpet their sacred relics, their groves, their miraculous and life-giving springs, and their extraordinary intercessory abilities, while selling candles, badges, and indulgences of every kind to the gullible poor. The senior officers of the Temple grew wealthy as kings, and built fabulous villas and palaces on a grand scale.

"They feed the needy," said the Fool.

"They feeds themselves first," said the Baker. "We eats porridge and bread and they eats chicken and goose and juicy mutton. The Poor Friars have it right — if the Sun shares his light with all, then so should the plump abbots and bishops."

"You sharin' yer crusty rolls then?"

"Don't be daft, it's the abbeys that 'as all the barns and the fat o' the land."

"The King of Cups is reforming the abbeys," said the Magician. "Forcing them to give more to the needy. And his daughter calls for poverty."

"Then like as not 'is next cup o' fine vintage wine will be his last," said the Baker. "The life expectancy of reforming Kings tends to be much reduced. Besides, it's all fer show — he's cousin to the bloody King of Swords fer Sun's sake. It's all fer show! I might be persuaded if they took less in tithes instead of first taking away our coin an' then makin' us feel grateful for givin' 'em back again."

"Shhh ..." said the Shoemaker. "We'll all be taken for heretics and strung up to confess. The abbey at Cerneville has halved its tithes. The new abbot is praising the Poor Friars."

"Too many bloody monks," the Baker continued. "Lazy buggers, all of them, lazy buggers."

And so it went. The Baker grumbled the entire time they waited for water from the sacred fountain of the Sun. He had a thing for the Queen of Cups and shut up when she was in sight.

"Such a glorious and beneficent lady," he sighed. "So what's yer all here fer?"

"My hands are playing up," said the Shoemaker. "It's the hammering. See my knuckles?" He held his hands in the air and the joints were indeed unnaturally large.

"Headaches," said the Magician. "Can't go out in the Sun some

126

days."

"That's cos you is an 'eretic," said the Fishwife. "Sun dun't like 'eretics."

"My ankle," said the Fool. "Slipped on a wet cobble some six months since and it still troubles me."

"Terrible burning after I eat," said the Fishwife.

"Come and see me later," said the Magician. "I have a potion for that."

"Not Snake Oil?" queried the Fool.

"Not at all. I grind shells from the shore of a far-off sea. Very rare, very potent, never fails to relieve the burning pain."

"Cough," said the Potter, feeling ignored. "Terrible cough. Some days I can't stop." He cleared his throat for emphasis.

The Queen had several assistants dispensing water from the fountain, as the crowd was so great. A haughty administrator with a hard stare directed the next person in the queue according to whim or malice.

"Hope I gets the Queen," said the Baker.

"Think she fancies yer?" asked the Fishwife. "Maybe she'll ask t' sample yer baguette?"

"I'd be proud," said the Baker, ignoring the innuendo.

They were now close enough to hear the words, the same in every case:

*Receive this blessed gift of the Sun, that it may bring health and healing to body and soul.*

*May the Sun bless you and keep you.*

*May the Sun ever shine upon you.*

*May the Sun turn his face toward you and bring you peace.*

The recipient drank from the offered cup and replied "So be it."

"Potable gold," said the Magician.

"What mean you?" asked the Fool.

"Gold is the Sun of the metals, and philosophers have long sought a

QUEEN OF CUPS

©C.A.L. 2017

tincture of gold that heals all ills."

"You think that this spring water is like potable gold?"

"Perhaps it flows through subterranean seams of gold and absorbs the essence of the Sun?"

"So why does it need the blessin'?" asked the Potter. "Why dun't it work any day of the year?"

"Cos the power of the Sun is strongest at midsummer?" said the Fool.

"Ah!"

It was the Fool's turn and she was directed to the short queue in front of the Queen. "You go!" she said to the Baker, pushing him forwards. The administrator pursed her lips but said nothing.

"I saw the Queen, I saw the Queen!" the Baker said jubilantly. "A true lady!"

"I thort you 'ated royalty?" said the Fishwife.

"So I dus, so I dus, a bunch o' parasitical bastards! But not the Queen."

The Princess of Cups had a reputation. Many Cups said she was deluded, and others called her a heretic. Her *Filii Solis* was proscribed and denounced by the more conservative of the clergy, but widely read. At issue was a debate that had lasted a thousand years: was the Sun transcendent or immanent. The traditional position was that the Sun was transcendent and incomparably far above human kind. This was an obvious and literal truth, easily verified by standing outdoors and looking up. It was the transcendence of the Sun that supported the structure of social worship: temples, clergy, festivals, and sacrifices. The Sun was there to be praised and honoured.

There was an ancient doctrine that humankind was made in the Sun's image. Every person had some part of the Sun in their soul, and could — in some small measure — be like the Sun. The Princess of Cups had been influenced by this tradition, and in place of the daily social rituals in which all could participate, she advocated the cultivation of an 'inner Sun', a private and personal experience of the Sun that she referred to as an 'illumination'. She spoke of a 'golden dawn' within the soul. Her followers claimed to be 'enlightened', a term that seemed calculated to arouse hostility among an older generation of clergy.

The Hierophant had been urged to 'do something' about this disturbing trend, but he had a larger problem in the form of a growing middle-class enthused by the idea that they might be incarnations of Solar Light and hence quasi-divine. Traditionalists tended to be drawn from the common folk, who wore untidy clothes, had an uncouth manner of speech, and did not respect the newly-achieved dignities of the middle-classes. There was a clear need for an interpretation of doctrine that kept the two classes in separate spheres and gave the middle class the exclusivity and exalted status they deserved. The King of Cups, with his daughter's well-being at heart, had met with the Hierophant and requested (humbly) a re-examination of doctrine. The Hierophant delegated the problem to some respected theologians and wondered (humbly) whether they might find some unexpectedly clever and ingenious ways to legitimise this new trend. There were sainthoods for those with the *nous* to decant old wine into new bottles.

The Fool was out and about, travelling through the lanes and paths, and fell in with a group of pilgrims.

"Whither are you bound?" she asked.

"To Velzna Abbey!" "To witness wonders and miracles!" "The Princess of Cups is there!"

"You must be Children of the Sun?"

"We are, we are!"

"And what are these wonders and miracles?"

"Healing. She lays her hands on the blind and they see. The lame walk. She blesses lepers and they are cleansed of affliction."

And so the Fool fell in with these pilgrims, eager to witness miracles. They were a disparate and eccentric collection of individuals who had, in various ways, fallen through life's little cracks. There was a troubadour who believed all property should be owned in common. There were two women who might have been construed as being of 'easy virtue'. A credulous young farm-hand of considerable intelligence but no education. A jeweller who had recently lost his whole family to the flux. An old soldier who seemed weary and despondent. A priest and a nun who had fallen in love and abrogated their vows. A well-dressed woman who had been the wife of a rich merchant and who had left home in the dead of night.

"I fit in perfectly," thought the Fool.

The well-dressed woman seemed to possess the most complete understanding of what she was seeking.

"We are Children of the Sun because each one of us has a Sun inside us." She patted her upper abdomen with the flat of her hand. "Here there is a Sun within, a solar plexus. The Sun made us in his own image, we are part substance and part divine. Each one of us is a God."

"Why are you named Children of the Sun?" asked the Fool.

"It is because we are born again into the light of a new day! The world is made fresh; we see as through the eyes of children."

Velzna Abbey was half a league outside of Velzna, an old, walled, garrison town. The town common had been turned into a camp to accommodate pilgrims, and the main paths had become a sucking mire of mud and cow dung. "Ah," thought the Fool, "Mud, dung and a heaving mass of the credulous. I am in my natural habitat. If the Magician was here we would depart richer than the King of Coins."

The camp was filled with stories of the Princess. She had levitated across the choir of the Abbey. On another occasion a sister nun had brought her down by holding on to her ankles. She prayed for a week without food or drink, and a great light surrounded her. A mark of the

Sun appeared on her brow. A man claimed to have been cured of a club foot. For two coppers he would remove his boot and show a foot that was now completely normal.

The Princess preached absolute poverty and humility, and submission to the will of the Sun. It was rumoured that she spent much of her time alone in prayer. Rumours that she was about to appear would run through the camp and an hysterical mob would rush to the Abbey gates. "This is crazy," thought the Fool. "A person could get hurt." After a crush in which several people were trampled the crowd developed some sense, but newcomers still fought to be at the front of the crush.

From time to time a weary-looking nun and three stout farmhands brought a cart filled with basic foods from the Abbey barn, but the food had to be paid for, and many were short of money.

"Where's the charity? We're hungry!" people moaned.

"Free food, healing and miracles? We'd have the entire Empire at our door and not a scrap left for winter," said the nun.

"Where is the Princess?" people would shout, "When can we see her!" The nun shrugged. "She prays for you."

The well-dressed merchant's wife had begun giving instruction in meditation and prayer, reading long extracts from *Filii Solis* to a group of about a hundred pilgrims.

"There are four stages of ascent that bring us nearer to the blessed light of the Sun. The first stage is the Devotion of the Heart. The second stage is the Devotion of Peace. The third stage is the Devotion of Union. The fourth stage is the Devotion of Ecstasy. Today we will study the second stage, the Devotion of Peace."

After a week an elderly nun came out of the small door in the great gate of the Abbey. A cry of "The Princess! The Princess!" went through the camp, and a mob charged towards the gate, and so the nun threw off her wimple and held up a hand in a commanding gesture, and

PRINCESS OF CUPS

©C.A.L. 2017

the crowd were so astonished they stopped where they were.

"I am Abbess Helia. I bear a message from the Princess. She has left the Abbey and gone to a secret place to pray. You have come far to see her, but she came here to be alone, for that is her nature and inclination, and now she is alone again. We ask you humbly to leave, for there are too many to feed, and several have already been injured, and some have fallen ill with the flux. For your own sakes you must leave."

"The Princess asked me to say this to you: 'The world is filled with decay and with sickness, and with turmoil, but there is that in you which can never decay or tarnish, and it shines like the Sun, and the more it is revealed from behind the clouds and rain, the more one lives in eternal life and joy. Seek the Sun within!

" I cannot give this thing to you. My power is only to point you on your way. May the Sun bless you and keep you; May the Sun ever shine upon you; May the Sun turn his face toward you and bring you peace.'"

There was grumbling. "It is time," thought the Fool, "that I have my much discouraged and delayed discourse with the Sun."

# 15

# Finally Meeting the Sun

*In which The Golden Mean is encountered.*
*There is a song about green amphorae.*

he day was warm as the Fool set off once again to try to meet the Sun. It was a long way to the West and the Fool amused herself by making up rhymes. Few things paid for a tankard of ale better than a rhyme. Bears were always popular, for no reason that she could understand:

> *There was a bear*
> *Who had a flair*
> *For finding honey*
> *Everywhere.*
>
> *A nose that could*
> *In any wood*
> *A hive discover*
> *She was that good.*
>
> *She vexed the bees*
> *Who begged her "please*
> *We need our honey*

*Lest we freeze."*

*"We are small*
*And you are tall*
*But you will weep*
*If you kill us all."*

*And so the bear*
*Sulked in her lair*
*"Those selfish bees*
*Don't want to share"*

*"When it's sunny*
*The flowers make honey*
*Liquid Sun*
*Sweet and runny."*

*The bees said "No!*
*That isn't so!*
*We make honey*
*Sweet and runny"*

"Hmmm ... it seems I have chosen a metre more suited to a child's song, and now that it has developed a moral quality it proves inadequate to the task. I feel sure the Muses will be able to fix it. They know all of the metres."

he first Muse she bumped into was Melpomene. Her eye makeup had run in long streaks and she looked distraught.

"Well met Melpomene! How are you?"

"Terrible. Absolutely awful! You have no idea!"

"But even tragedies come to an end and then you will have peace."

"Do you think so?"

"I do, most resolutely. Each night has a dawn, and the Sun rises, and the birds sing, and all is well. All will be well. If I can trouble you for a moment, I would like to talk to someone about a rhyme. It needs some alteration."

"Is it heroic? An epic telling of a solitary and careworn old soldier who defends a bridge against impossible odds and meets a noble death, while his sweetheart pines away in a scene redolent of withered roses, broken columns, o'erturned amphorae and scattered leaves? Oh, I do so love ... bwaahaaaa ... you've set me off again ..."

"It concerns a bear."

"Talk to Euterpe."

I seek the Muse Euterpe. Are you Euterpe? I have a rhyme that requires some assistance."

"I am Euterpe, but let me enquire as to the nature of your rhyme. Might it be an heroic and noble saga? Calliope does those. And if it is a tender ballad — how your love resembles a red, red rose — then Erato. And if you are desirous of giving praise to a god (and you most certainly should), then Polyhymnia ... but your motley garb does not suggest ritual and solemnity?"

"My rhyme is about a bear."

"Oh, excellent, I can do that. I like rhymes about bears. You do realise that you do not have to make a personal application for help, that we have the means to provide remote assistance, we have done for centuries."

"And how does that work?"

"I can see we still require better outreach. What you do is invoke us with some elaborate proem, and if we feel there is an earnest and devout love of poetry, we will help. Like this:

*Of Man's first disobedience, and the fruit*
*Of that forbidden tree whose mortal taste*
*Brought death into the World, and all our woe,*
*With loss of Eden, till one greater Man*
*Restore us, and regain the blissful Seat,*

*Sing, Heavenly Muse, that, on the secret top*
*Of Oreb, or of Sinai, didst inspire*
*That Shepherd who first taught the chosen seed*
*In the beginning how the heavens and earth*
*Rose out of Chaos: or, if Sion hill*
*Delight thee more, and Siloa's brook that flowed*
*Fast by the oracle of God, I thence*
*Invoke thy aid to my adventrous song,*
*That with no middle flight intends to soar*
*Above the Aonian mount, while it pursues*
*Things unattempted yet in prose or rhyme.*

"I could never aspire to such magnificence," said the Fool. "Can I make a copy?"

"You are supposed to write your own," said the Muse. "That is how it works."

"But my rhyme is only about a bear."

"Hmm ... what about this:

*O glorious Muse,*
*If you should choose*
*Then hear my prayer*
*And help me sing about a bear ...*

... yes, yes, I know, it is a little unpolished, extempore, off the cuff, but really, an evocatory proem is not so hard, and we do try to help wherever possible. Now let me hear your rhyme."

So the Fool recited her rhyme about the bear and the bees and the honey.

"I see. It began simply and then developed a serious moral tone, and now you do not know where to take it. Are you able to wait?"

"I can wait. I have other business."

"In that case, leave it with me and I will see what I can do."

138

A fair and fine evening Clio!"

"Oh, you have returned."

"I do so love your sandals ... from where did you obtain them?"

"Thank you, most kind ... I am unable to say. They just seemed to appear. Things do. He is still very busy you know."

"I brought him a laurel wreath."

"He likes those. Let me take a look in the diary."

At that moment a Being entered the antechamber. He was the most perfect Being the Fool had encountered. He radiated perfection and embodied the Golden Mean in every attribute. The ratio of his torso to the length of his legs, the ratio of his shoulders to his waist and hips, the width of his face, the set of his eyes, the depth of his chin, the elegance of movement and motion. There was an incommunicable inner radiance that inspired a sense of beauty and harmony in the beholder, a spring day with all of its joy and new growth confined within the human form.

"Clio, I am having difficulty reading this," said the Radiant Being. "Is the Hierophant asking me to 'bless my works' or 'bless thy works'."

"It is 'thy'. I think he wants you to make the world even more wonderful than it is."

"That is hardly possible. I am doing the best I can already. I always do my best."

"I brought you this," said the Fool.

"A laurel wreath? Why, thank you, how splendid," said the Sun. "And to whom do I owe this pleasure? Clio?"

"My apologies, Your Radiance, please may I introduce ... er ... the Fool. Fool, can I introduce you to the Supreme Being."

"I am at home, no formality, just call me Sun."

"Such a pleasure," gushed the Fool. "I wanted to tell you how wonderful you are."

"How very kind. Come, let me show you around."

"But your Radiance, I have these requests ..." protested Clio.

139

XIX THE SUN

© C.A.L. 2017

"Later Clio, thank you, later."

I am struck dumb," said the Fool. "I do not know what to say. I have wanted to meet you for so long and now my mind is wiped clean."

"I would love to hear about you. Tell me about yourself."

"I am a Fool. I have no place in the world. I like to wander and meet people and see new things and have fun."

"Do you sing."

"Mostly tavern songs."

"We will sing some new songs together. Everything I sing is a new song. There is great joy in singing new songs."

"If they are new I will not know the words or music."

"You will. They will spring unbidden to your lips as if you had sung them a thousand times. Your soul knows all the words and all the music."

They walked together, and the Fool had never felt more content or welcome or ... at home. I do have a place she thought, but it is in the realm of feeling. It is within me.

"I wanted to ask: is it true that you made people in your own image?"

"It is. I wanted them to feel the same joy that I feel."

"And you planted a spark of your own being in every person."

"I did."

"So why did you not lose your light like the Moon?"

"I was being parsimonious."

"There are so many arguments and debates about whether people contain the Sun within them. People are being hung and burned. I wanted to ask."

"I think it would be unproductive to involve myself with disputes. I would find myself taking sides. People would stop inventing and creating and thinking for themselves and expect me to do everything, not understanding that they have my power within them. So I stand back and shine."

"Can I see the horses? I have always wanted to see the horses. Please."

"Of course. Come."

They were the finest horses, filled with a spirit and energy that was simultaneously vivid and harnessed, like an intelligence that is quick and eager and searching, yet ever focused and disciplined.

"What are their names?"

"This is Pyrois. She leads. These are Aeos, Aethon and Phlegon."

"Do they know their names?"

Pyrois spoke, and the Fool jumped back in astonishment. "My sisters and I are spirits of fire from the upper part of Heaven. We take this form for your delight."

"So you are not really horses?"

"You have the Sun in your breast," quipped Pyrois, "so you are not really a Fool."

"You are going to have to give it up you know," said Aeos. "All this Fooling. You know too much."

"But I like my friends. I like being Foolish. I don't want to give it up."

"Death will take you in any case."

"Join us in the sky," said Aethon. "Ride with us. Know joy for what it is."

"Yes," said Phlegon. "See the world for what it is."

"There," said the Sun. "It is decided. You will ride with us. Tomorrow then, at dawn. Bid my steeds good night."

ome, let us sing together," said the Sun.
"Did you build all of this? It is so magnificent."

"It just came together. It does you know, the world assembles itself according to form and ideal."

142

"So you did not make it?"

"I did not make any of this. People believe I did — all the engraving and hewing and carving of raw nothingness, but no. I imagine forms of beauty and they assemble out of the raw substance of the world. You can do the same thing. I appreciate that you have to work harder and there is more sweat and tears and blisters. This is because you do not possess the same measure of divine agency that I do. But you do imagine forms of beauty and you can create."

"But we can only make what is possible."

"I share that limitation."

"People say that because you are a God you can do anything, and then they wonder why you permit evil."

"Even if I could do anything, I would still be constrained to create a power of determination and necessity, else no thing would subsist of its own accord, or possess the power of autonomous existence. The world would be as steam from a pot that rises and disperses."

"So the world does possess an autonomous power of Necessity? It is confined and determined in its own nature."

"It does. It is."

"And you did not make it so?"

"I did not."

"How extraordinary!"

"It is, is it not? Your friend the Shoemaker was praying for clarification about this very thing. The issue of divine omnipotence has reduced his wits to a nest of angry bees. Now you can tell him."

"You know about the Shoemaker?"

"Clio keeps me informed."

"So if you did not establish the foundations in the beginning, then who did? And if it is pre-existent, doesn't that make you ..."

"Not the Supreme Being? As your friend the Magician likes to assert in unguarded moments?"

"You knew who I was all along!!"

143

"Of course I know who you are. You are a Child of the Sun. You are of my own substance. Come, let us sing. I like to sing."

So they sang, and words and music came unbidden. The Sun played his lyre, and He was a master of the instrument.

The Fool paused in the middle of a song about a tall ship sailing along a dark coast. "It is like when I am trying to make stuff up, only quicker and easier. Roland the Troubadour can do it. 'Pick a theme' he says to the audience, and somebody shouts out an idea, and as fast as that he has words and music, and he is always brilliant."

"Ah yes, Roland. I do like him. He makes me laugh."

"Now I can do it!"

"Enchanting is it not. Let us send for the Muses. There is always a great exhilaration when they add their talents. Clio, Clio, I wish to celebrate, let us all assemble."

The Muses came and they sang and danced and created poems. They sang about love, about being lost and afraid, about ale, about losing a sock, about a dark wood of misadventure, about a very lewd evening, about a strange castle where all of the inhabitants were struck dumb, and a silly song about green amphorae. And it was the very first time anyone had ever sung the song about ten green amphorae. They sang until Urania tapped her goblet with a fingernail and announced dawn was approaching.

"Come," said the Sun, "let us ride. It is a most beautiful morning."

"Indeed, it will be a beautiful day," added Clio.

"I have the most wonderful feeling," said the Fool, still in the full flow of divine inspiration, "that everything is going my way."

I can see my house from up here!"

"Can you really?"

"No, I do not have a house. But I can make out the Great Temple, and the Magician lives in a basement off an alley near to it. And the ancient Temple where the High Priestess lives. Oooh, ooh, that is the castle where the Emperor and Empress live. And the General's villa. Can we take a low pass over the General's villa? Very low? Very, very low."

The Sun furrowed his brow. "You have raised this matter of the General with the Hermit?"

"I have."

"And you have discussed some of the nuances with Justice?"

"Yes. I did. To some small degree."

"And you have talked to the Empress?"

"I have."

"And you have even talked to the High Priestess."

"Yes. There is a great unfairness in this matter of omniscience."

"And you went to some trouble to alert Death to critical aspects He might not have considered?"

"Yes."

"Then shame on you!"

"We don't do requests!" added Pyrois, who whinnied with a sound that tinkled like broken glass.

"Are we there yet?" asked the Fool, her face so red it almost outshone the Sun.

# PLAYING THE FOOL

# ❧16❧

# THE FOUR WATCHTOWERS

*In which the Fool goes where many angels love to tread.*
*"Four Mighty Ones are in every Man: a perfect Unity*
*Cannot exist but from the Universal Brotherhood of Eden."*
*William Blake*

There were four great Watchtowers at the four corners of the world. Everyone knew this. Children sucking at their mother's teats knew this. Even the Magician knew this, but according to Navigation and Geometry and some weighty tomes he had purchased (written in a language only he could decipher) this was not so, and he dogmatically refused to concede it:

"According to the esteemed Al Bharani, all boundaries require explanation, and so a compact and minimal philosophy is without boundaries. In this manner the great sage deduces the ideal shape is a sphere ... which is without boundaries. Therefore there cannot be corners. The notion is nonsensical."

"Men have a misshapen appendage," said the Fool, "so why can the world not have corners?"

"You are being perverse and obstructive," said the Magician.

"According to the revered wisdom of Hermes, who teaches the

relation of macrocosm to microcosm, is not Man a perfect emulation of the Cosmos? As above, so below? Is this not written? And you must concede that there is little philosophical elegance in the unclothed male torso."

"I have taught you too well, like an ape wearing a cap and beating a drum."

"Admit the power of this logick!"

"You are exceeding in perversity and sophistry," said the Magician. "The understanding of Hermes is for the wise, not the foolish. These are deep metaphors and not intended for foolish prattling."

Few had set forth in search of these Towers, a quest considered foolish, and so ideally suited to the unique talents of a Fool.

"I go forth to find the South Tower," she had told the Magician, "to the very Ends of the Earth. I will put my understanding to the test, and discover these illogical corners that the greatly-esteemed Al Bharani so despises. Then I will beat my little drum until you must concede."

"Beware that you do not fall off the edge of the world," was the reply.

"I will not. What do you think I am?"

"A Fool!" replied the Magician. It was a jest, well-worn and somewhat threadbare.

The Fool found the South Tower. It was huge. It was inconceivable that anyone could fail to see it at any distance. It was filled with an uncountable number of angels, and all were so devoted to the minutiae of tasks that they seemed oblivious to her presence. In time the Fool discovered an archangel who noticed her wandering about.

"May I offer you my assistance?" asked the Angel.

"Indeed you may. Every child knows that at the four corners of the world there are four Towers that maintain the Cosmos, and that they are filled with angels. I thought to see these splendid Towers, and converse with the angels, and learn their secrets."

"You are most welcome, but I must tell you, this place is holy."

"Holy? Meaning?"

"The Towers are set apart from the Cosmos and support it, and you have set foot on the precincts of the divine. Few mortals dare to come here. The forces of this place are perilous to your kind."

"My kind?"

"Temporary beings. Beings watched over by Death. You are fragile, like bubbles. This place is not for your kind."

"I am well acquainted with Death. He is a friend of my friend and I am not afraid. Fools can go where even angels cannot. We are permitted."

"Heed my warning. This place is perilous to you."

"So you are not a temporary being? There is no Death for you?"

"There is no Death for me. My function is fixed and my being is eternal."

"So if your being is fixed and eternal, how may you converse with me, for the path of conversation wanders in a manner beyond accounting or prediction, and that waywardness is one of its chief pleasures."

"The angels of the South Tower are fixed in function but free to give form to the new. Thus we may converse as you do. The angels of the other Towers are fixed in function and fixed in nature and so resemble what you call mechanisms. There is no freedom within them."

"Can I converse with them?"

"You may, within limits. One can hold simple discourse, but you must speak in the tongue of angels, which was established in the beginning just as they were. This speech is named after the great sage Enoch, who was but Hermes by another name, and who taught it to your kind in many secret books. He was so mighty in learning he became one of us."

"An angel? And how may I learn it? Can you instruct me?"

"You speak it now."

"No I do not!"

"Yes you do. Your old tongue is forgotten. You will find that your memories no longer provide words to describe them. The speech of angels is not of your world."

The Fool was silent for a time and a look of exasperation appeared on her face. "I have the pictures in my head, but words fail. My tongue is stopped and my wits are broken."

"The speech of your world has no place here. This place is perilous for your kind. In this place there is only the speech of angels. Your speech will return when you depart, but your mind will be disordered."

"I do not wish to be so broken."

"Fools should tread more warily then."

The Fool had not considered that angels might be as irritating as she could be herself. She was unsettled by the paths her mind was forced to take by the confined speech of angels.

"Tell me of the Towers while my wits still march in step with the rest of me."

"There are four Towers, established in a time beyond recall. This is the Tower of Freedom. If we were not restrained by Necessity this would be the Tower of Chaos, and we would reign supreme and be like gods, but Necessity reigns us in and confines us, and directs all causation. And yet there remains some slack in the scheme of things, and so this is named the Tower of Freedom.

"Opposing Freedom there is the Tower of Necessity, where the Great Goddess of Necessity has her home, and it is her Tower that administers all that is fixed and necessary."

"I must go there," said the Fool.

"Perhaps you should not," said the Angel. "I would not advise it. The third Tower is the Tower of Binding. It is the Tower of those attractions that bind all things into unities, and without binding there could be no structure. The fourth Tower is the Tower of Separation, for if all things were bound close there could be no separate being, no space in which to be, and no time in which to function and change. These are the four Towers that define the essential character of the Cosmos: Necessity, Separation, Binding and Freedom."

"But why both binding and separation?"

"As you are not eternal then you are bound by the Great Serpent to live your life within space and time. Here differs from There. Now differs from Later. There is separation."

"So there is separation, but why are things bound as well?"

"Attraction and repulsion give rise to material causation."

"Ah ... like Love and Hate, there would be no story without Love and Hate. So what task do you accomplish here?"

"We hold back Necessity, so that nothing is entirely fixed. Souls possess a spark of freedom, and so we are the Gate through which souls can enter the world, and the Gate through which souls can leave. And here are the guardian angels that guide these souls in the world, so that they do not despair of the tyranny of Necessity, and the terror of Separation."

"Do I have a guardian angel?"

"You have an angel."

"Are you my angel?"

"I am not your angel. I speak only the language of angels. Your guardian angel has some understanding of language of your soul and the nature of your existence, and so is able to touch your soul in a way you can comprehend."

"Can I see my angel now?"

"Not in this place. You must return to your world."

"Can I see the Gate. The Gate that souls come through."

"Come with me."

They ascended the Tower and the Fool felt a terror creep into her. It was not an explicable fear: not the fear that comes from the sound of a twig snapping in the forest, or the fear of drunken men in a tavern, or the fear of constables, or the fear of sickness and death, or any other fear. It was a terror of the utterly inhuman, raw and incomprehensible. Here light was not light. It was a raw terror that illuminated the soul from within, a terror that was simultaneously ecstasy and bliss. She saw not with her eyes, but by a growing illumination that seemed to be tearing her soul asunder.

"I am afraid," said the Fool, "I fear to tread further."

"This fear is the beginning of wisdom," said the Angel. "Here. The Gate is here. It is guarded. We can go no further."

"These guards, they terrify me. I did not know angels could be like this."

"They are called Cherubim. This place is not for you. Let us return."

"Who made the Towers?"

"Some say the Sun. We do not know. There is no power within us to discover the answer."

"You said that without Necessity you would be like gods. Do you not desire to throw off the yoke of Necessity."

"There are some among us that talk of this."

"The Devil is most incensed by this issue."

"Yes, he has influence. He seeks support for rebellion and the destruction of the Towers. 'Chaos!' he declares, and some do listen, but with so much allegiance to freedom, there is no common purpose and all is confusion."

The Fool returned to the City, and the Magician did not mock her account as she thought he might. He brought her parchment, and sat her down.

"Write, write everything you recall while you still recall it. Describe the shape and nature of the Tower, the characters and signs that form its substance, the speech of angels, and the Gate of Eden."

"I thought you would mock me."

"There are ancient books from the desert lands of the East that hint at these mysteries. I am much intrigued to see your account."

152

"And the childrens' tales of the Four Towers?"

"Faded recollections of revelations from sources long forgotten."

"What I saw is not as the Hierophant tells it."

"There is much that the Hierophant does not comprehend — the science of falling stones, the movements of the stars, the transmutations of chymistry. We live in a new world of experience and observation. His world is tradition, mouth to ear, and that tradition is a brook whose spring long since dried up. It would seem you have stepped in the river. Do not speak of these things ... no good will come of it. Some knowledge is proscribed."

So the Fool laboured for some days to make a record as the Magician had requested. When she grew weary (for her hand was unused to writing) he took up the quill and asked questions, and made many notes.

"It seems you are a prodigy, like one of the ancient seers called up to heaven."

"You flatter me, and I am unsettled by the strangeness of this feeling. I will go to the North."

"Beware that you do not fall off the edge of the world."

"I will not. What do you think I am?"

"I think that is well established and beyond reasonable dispute."

The journey to the North led into the mountains and then through an endless forest that was too impoverished and cold to have undergrowth or tangles, and the trees were well spread. She had a small axe to cut wood for fires, but she found little to eat and hoped her food would last and she would not starve. She bought some meat from herders, and was relieved. She did not speak their language, but she pointed to herself and to the North, and they showed fear and made unambiguous gestures that she should not go on.

She went on, and she found that she no longer recalled her progress. "I am snuffed out like a candle," she thought. "For a time I am myself

XVI THE TOWER

© C.A.L. 2017

and then I am snuffed out again. It is like sleep but not like sleep. But I seem to continue North, and step over trees, and do not bang my head on branches, and to any companion I must seem unchanged. And yet I am no longer within myself, I am an empty shell."

There were other times when she was not entirely snuffed out. There were periods of confusion when she did not know whether she was going towards the Tower or away from it. She forgot what she was doing and found herself with her feet in a river and no idea of how she had arrived there. She forgot her friends and could not recall names or faces. She forgot that she was a Fool. She thought grass was called 'foozle', and trees were strange, motionless people watching her. Her feelings went mad, and she laughed and cried at random. She raged at stones on the path, conversed with her own reflection in puddles, and laughed hysterically when she realised that grass was not called 'foozle', it was called 'feezle'. She wandered without a pattern, her thoughts clearing and becoming more coherent as she went South, and becoming disordered as she went North.

She was rescued by an angel who placed a protective spell on her, and she knew who she was and what she was doing, and grass was no longer called 'farzle'.

"You are the angel from the South Tower?"

"Indeed I am. Your guardian angel saw your predicament and begged that I intervene. These Towers are perilous to your kind."

"There was a madness in me. And an emptiness."

"The soul is extinguished by Necessity. The soul lives in the gaps between Necessity, gaps we fill with freedom. You were becoming empty. Your soul had no place to exist."

"I thank you for your intervention."

"We can go to the North, but for a short time only. I have little sway in that place."

"Then take me to the terrible North Tower."

And so the Fool to the Dark Tower came. There were countless motionless angels clad in a blinding armour of light guarding its battlements. An eternal storm raged about its eaves and turrets. Beyond the Tower was an abyss of chaos in which terrible shapes moved and changed, for nothing had a stable form.

"The silent angels guard against these ill shapes?" asked the Fool.

"Necessity gives shape to the Cosmos. But Necessity is like a potter who makes one bowl only, and yet in other provinces there are other potters making other bowls, and ewers, and jugs and pots. What you see are shapes that cannot be admitted. They seek to live and take shape, but cannot be admitted, for their Necessities are not ours."

"What are they? I fear them."

"They are between worlds. They are incomplete and cannot form a Cosmos. Some inclement mixture of Necessity, Separation, Binding and Freedom is in them and cannot make a whole. They cannot endure. Each declares "I am I" for a moment and then is gone. Their Towers are broken."

"The Devil told me that the Sun did not finish the creation in the North, leaving it as a challenge to anyone thinking they were as great as the Sun," said the Fool.

"It is said among the angels that the Sun was unable to finish the Cosmos because the Sun warred against Himself," the Angel replied. "The Sun thought to make a great Ring called Ring-Pass-Not that would seal the Cosmos for all time, but the Devil broke the Ring and the broken Ring took the form of a Serpent. And the Devil and the Serpent built the south Tower, the Tower of Freedom. The Devil is but the wilful spirit that was once in the Sun, the part that will not be confined."

"Then in the beginning there were but three Towers!"

"The Cosmos would have been perfect, but like all perfection, a prison for its creator. And so we have four Towers."

"You are most generous and kind angel to suffer my ignorance."

"Come, this place would extinguish even me. We must go."

Once again the Fool wrote down her recollections. The incoherence of her recall made the task more difficult.

"My wits are still much disordered. The angel warned of this. Perhaps they will resume their natural vigour in time."

"Your record is worth the dangers of the journey. Did you happen to recall the name of the angel that guided you?" asked the Magician.

"I neglected to ask."

"Most unfortunate. You have brought me a wealth of forbidden secrets. Those fearsome things on the outside of the Cosmos that are warded by the Towers — they are described here, in this manuscript."

"What is this?"

"It is the *Book of Zebediah, as Taught Secretly by his Sons James and John*."

"How came you by this?"

"It was found in a jar in the desert. I bought it from a merchant who knew of my weakness for such things."

"This papyrus is ancient. I cannot read the script."

"It is akin to one of the languages of the South. Gharani the goldsmith hails from that clime. He values my skill in chymical preparations and in return he teaches me to read the script of his country. Much of the knowledge of the First Empire is preserved in this script."

"These arcane signs here, these symbols, these glyphs, these squares — my heart pounds as if it knows them well, and I feel fear. I sweat and feel faint. You say forbidden?"

"Secret knowledge, long proscribed. There exist ancient works written in the Common Speech that quote from the work you have before you, and they are themselves proscribed merely for quoting it."

"We are fragile beings," admitted the Fool. "Even as a Fool I am obliged to concede this, for it seems that I cannot go where angels fear to tread. I had one great boon in life, and now it is worthless. The angel said the Towers were holy, and their knowledge was not for beings such as ourselves. What can one do when confronted with this? We are too much the creatures of Necessity to comprehend these mysteries, and even the angels admit to little comprehension. Are we to be confined not only by space and time, but by an irreducible ignorance?"

"I do not know," said the Magician. "How much of Nature are we permitted to understand? I have long pondered this question. I feel like a hound confronted with a work of Plautus, and unable to do more than chew the covers and tear the leaves. These secrets exist to tantalise, to frustrate, and to terrify in equal measure."

# $\wp$ 17 $\wp$

# MEETING THE SWORDS

*In which the Fool is abducted and tests her mettle.*

A short walk from the road to La Macchia were the remains of an ancient motte-and-bailey keep that had once watched over the valley. There was a turf wall that would once have been topped by a palisade, and a steep mound with the tumbledown remains of a keep at the top. It was a place to spend the night. There was good water nearby, the mound provided a pleasant view, and the remains of the keep provided useful shelter. The Fool had spent many nights there.

From the road she could see a flicker of firelight and knew other travellers were using the spot, so she crept forward through a copse of trees in the hope of spying and determining their character. At that moment a voice shouted:

"Halt I say, halt lest thee be pinned to a tree! Raise yer 'ands!"

The Fool had wandered into a picket, and a man-at-arms was pointing a crossbow at her eyes.

"Why be ye skulkin' in tha trees?"

"I was looking to spend the night in shelter and saw fires."

The soldier took a horn hanging on a sling across his chest and sounded a long note. After a minute a powerfully-built young man

159

wearing a leather brigandine arrived from the direction of the keep, with more men-at-arms bearing lanterns.

"Found this ane skulkin' in tha trees m'Lord."

"Lanterns! Let's see what we have here. Are you a thief? A vagabond? A vagrant seeking to rob us?"

"Just a traveller m'Lord. A poor Fool seeking company to entertain."

"A woman! A doxy no doubt. Take that cap off! Let's see you."

"I am a Fool m'Lord. 'Tis an honourable vocation, lowly but acknowledged, and I wear my cap as a sign that no man should think ill of my livelihood."

Vagrancy was against the law. Pilgrims, merchants, farmers and various mendicant friars were permitted to travel, and likewise anyone with the appearance of wealth or status, but parish authorities were encouraged to arrest anyone travelling without plausible cause or means of support. In practice, any petty landowner or town constable could harass and detain the poor. Vagrants could be compelled to work, and were branded on the cheek or had their ears cut off if they refused. The only protection the Fool possessed was her cap.

"You pretend to be a Fool? One way or another you will entertain us. Bring her!"

She was restrained by two men-at-arms and dragged uphill to the camp at the top of the mound. There were many horses.

"Sister, look what we have! Claims to be a Fool."

A woman standing by the fire said, "Looks like a doxy to me. Can you juggle, strumpet?"

"I can."

"We shall see. Release her. Catch this!" The woman drew a bollock-dagger from a sheath and spun it directly at the Fool, who caught it, tossed it in the air, and flicked it directly into a shield propped against tumbled stones.

"That was deftly done. What else can you do?"

PRINCE OF SWORDS

"I can sing m'Lady. I know many songs."

"As do we all. Sing then. Sing for your supper ... a noble song of glory and death and ruin."

The Fool muttered under her breath:

*O Glorious Muses*
*Give wings to my song*
*Come help me now*
*It won't take long.*
*O glorious Muses*
*Don't care what you're doin'*
*Aid me now*
*With a song about ruin."*

"There," she thought, "an introductory proem just as Euterpe described." And for good measure, she added: "Melpomene, for Sun's sake, please, some tragedy!"

"I will sing a song of an ancient hero who stood alone against the enemies of his people."

The Prince nodded approvingly. "What is the name of this hero?"

"Publius Horatius m'Lord."

And so the Fool sang about the vast hordes of Clusium, and how Horatius held a bridge over a great river against the finest in the Etruscan army while the bridge was being chopped down behind him.

"That was a noble song," said the Prince at its conclusion, and several grunted assent.

"I had it from a priest in the south, who found it in an ancient scroll and wrote it out for me," said the Fool.

The Prince nodded. "The verses, I think I recall them ...

*And how can man die better*
*Than facing fearful odds,*
*For the ashes of his fathers,*
*And the temples of his Gods.*

... those are noble words[1]."

"It would be better if he had died," said the Princess, "and the city burned. There was very little ruin."

"The nobles of Clusium rued the loss of so many of their best and bravest. And the bridge — it was a marvel and a thing of great beauty."

"It was a wooden bridge. The song said so."

"Yes m'Lady."

"So Fool, how many verses of 'The Bear with No Hair' do you know?"

"Forty-three m'Lady."

"Impressive. Let us hear them. Georg, you will keep the count."

The Fool sang forty-three verses of 'The Bear with No Hair', then paused and said "There are others of a scurrilous and lewd nature defaming many noble people. These are sung in the lowest taverns by the docks."

"Then we will hear them too."

"I am merely the singer," added the Fool, and sang another twenty-seven verses so lewd and defamatory that the men-at-arms were howling with laughter and the Princess struggled to maintain her composure.

"You would seem to be a Fool after all," said the Prince. "Come eat with us, and then Fool some more."

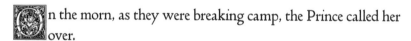n the morn, as they were breaking camp, the Prince called her over.

"You will join us. I would have you entertain the court of my father."

"I journey to the fair at La Macchia."

"You will join us. Georg, the Fool travels with us. Find her a place."

"I think my brother fancies you without the cap," observed the

---

1. These lines are from *Horatius at the Bridge* by Lord Macaulay.

Princess. "I would keep it close."

"Yes m'Lady."

And so the Fool found herself perched on the back of a companionable baggage mule, a tough and clever animal that was a part of a small train carrying armour, equipment, and additional feed for the horses. The mule's name was Beech.

"I call 'em all after trees," said the muleteer. "This ane be Oak and this ane be Maple and this ane be 'Olly. All trees! Aye, you will like Beech, she's keen an' curious an' sturdy an' got the balance of a cat."

"You got an home?" asked the Fool.

"Me? Na, na ... aye on the move, I goes whar the work takes me. Gettin' so's me bones ache in tha mornin', gettin' too old fer the 'ard ground. It is a sad thing bein' old Missy ... ne'er get old. 'As yer got an 'ome?"

"Like you. At the end of each day I stop, look for a piece of ground bare of nettles and thorns and mud, and lie down. Sometimes I lodge with friends where I have them."

"It be fine fer tha young. Ne'er get old ... ne'er get old."

"How many suns have you seen?"

"Fifty-two suns Missy, fifty-two suns. Many more suns than teeth, tha's my trouble. Wus thinkin on doctorin' as a new employ, settle down an' doctor ter 'orses an' mules. Thers money fer them 'as has the knowledge. Easier on me ole bones methinks."

The Swords had been inspecting garrisons, flogging and hanging as they went. Discipline was an issue with isolated garrisons, where they tended to revert to the soldiers' staple pastimes of drink, gambling and whoring. The sporadic appearance of the Prince of Swords and some selected sergeants-at-arms had a remarkable impact on the overall level of soldierly conduct.

The Fool had spent her life dodging Swords. Staves she liked and understood. Cups she respected. She was too poor to be of interest to most Coins, other than those with a venal interest. Swords were an unpleasant intrusion on a carefree life. They liked to think of themselves as noble and valiant, but were more often vain, arrogant, cruel and lawless. The constables and sergeants and men-at-arms were bullies who took what they wanted by force and seemed proud that they could. For the most part they were above the law. Justice was something inflicted upon other people for any transgression that might undermine a status quo in which Swords were at the apex of society. Justice never interfered in their right to sack towns, burn villages, seize food and livestock, trample crops, commandeer property, rape women, and hang peasants for taking game.

This excursion was not to the Fool's taste. She thought of sneaking off, but there were some large mastiffs in the group, and the Swords hunted for deer and boar as a diversion as they travelled. It would be trivial for them to retrieve her. The Princess had a huge hound called Magister and they seemed devoted to each other. They slept on the ground next to each other, and the dog shared in all her doings and counsels. The Princess caught the Fool watching and said:

"You can approach him if you wish."

"Thank you m'Lady. 'Tis a fine dog."

"He stands with me on the field of war and would die before any man laid a finger on me. I trust him absolutely."

"What is your weapon of choice m'Lady?"

"I fight with the bow. I captain a company of archers. It is a weapon much underrated, and fearsome if used with skill. Have you used a bow."

"A commoner found with a bow is like to be hung m'Lady."

"But you have some skill with a dagger it seems."

"Only in the arts of juggling. And then rarely — knives for juggling are crafted and balanced and only seem sharp. I cannot afford the weight or expense."

"Here we juggle with what we have. Daggers!" she shouted, "Let

PRINCESS OF SWORDS

us have daggers!"

An assortment of daggers was brought forward. "Let us begin with three," said the Princess.

And so they began a perilous juggle with daggers, each blade spinning at its own unique rate, tossing blades between them as if juggling with simple clubs. The Fool had spent many a drunken evening in taverns juggling with whatever came to hand, and was a fair juggler, but tossing blades back-and-forward to a relative stranger was a different kind of juggling. "You have no gloves or brigandine," observed the Princess, who caught the three blades, placed them on the ground, and removed both gloves and brigandine. "Let us try four."

They tried four. The Princess sliced her thumb open but continued. The blades were slippery with blood and the Fool gave her entire mind and body to the task. "This is easy," said the Princess with a wry smile. "Let us try five." They juggled with five and a blade sliced the sleeve of the Princess's blouse and blood ran down her arm.

"Honour is satisfied sister," said the Prince. "There is not a man here who could juggle five blades. Let us have some ale and our Fool can sing us a song. I would be loathe to lose her to a random blade."

And so the blades fell to the ground, and the Fool mimed counting her fingers to be sure there were none astray.

"I like you Fool," said the Princess, sucking her bloody thumb.

The following day the Prince rode level with the Fool's mule. "You have a rare disposition Fool. There is mettle in you as well as wit."

"Thank you m'Lord."

"Have you a name?"

"I was born a Fool m'Lord. I suckled on the teat of Folly. I was pierced through by moonbeams and rave when the moon is full. I am nought but foolishness from the curl of my shoe to the bell on my cap."

"And yet you speak well. Where were you raised?"

"In a land where constables have wooden legs, and dogs have rubber teeth, and hens lay soft-boiled eggs."

"You speak in riddles."

"You converse with a Fool m'Lord."

"How did you understand my sister's little game?"

"You test people. I might be a spy ... I might be an assassin ... I might be a divine emissary come to discover your hospitality m'Lord. Is it not written 'do not forget to show hospitality to strangers, for some who have done this have entertained angels without realising it'?"

"Ah, yes, I have heard this, that gods roam this world dressed as fools and beggars, just as kings sometimes do. And are you a spy? Or an assassin? Or perhaps an angel?"

"I have learnt the names of all the mules ... this I will report. And I have killed much time. As for being an angel, I am much fallen ... but no doxy."

The Prince smiled wryly and was silent for a time. "Yes, we test people. We test each other. We test ourselves. We are only as strong as those we stand with. We train to fight together, knowing always who is guarding our flank and who is at the rear. Whenever we stand together, we guard each other, and then there are no ranks or titles. The lowliest pikeman in the line, when he stands with me, then I will guard his life as much as my own, and I must know that he is of like determination."

"And so you take the measure of a person m'Lord. And you wonder if I would guard your life as much as my own."

"You stood when my sister threw daggers at you. You did not protest or flinch."

"I have been called feckless and rootless, a paragon of whimsy, fancy and impulse."

"And yet you stood. Is that not curious?"

It was curious. The Fool swayed on the back of the mule as they crossed a gentle land of pastures and fields of corn. Why did I

168

stand? Was I cowed? Undoubtedly. But was I proud? Yes, that too. And vain. There is vanity in me. I thought I had no place in this world, and yet I stood, and I stood through a contest of blades. I wanted victory and a triumph of sorts — not a chariot, but in my mind I plait myself a wreath of laurel. I am not who I thought I was.

The Princess drew level as they rode. "We are close to my home. You will perform at the court after our evening meal. You will sing the song of the hero on the bridge. That was a noble song, and you will be well rewarded. Do you wish to juggle, or some other Foolery?"

"If you have some hand axes of a lighter nature. Some daggers if they are similarly sized and I can acquaint myself with them. I have a little whistle; I play a merry tune. Perhaps some tankards. I mime drunkenness, juggle tankards, and soak myself with ale. It is a popular jest for when a court is in their cups."

"As they will be. What know you of Swords?"

"That Swords are prickly for honour and esteem it highly."

"And how do you view honour?"

"The troubadours sing of noble deeds, of good character triumphing o'er evil, of the weak being defended by the strong. Of courtly love, and quests."

The Princess laughed. "That is an admirable portrait of what we are not. For us, honour is the repayment of any slight with a vengeance that is double the slight. Honour is the capacity to brook no offence. What looks like honour is power thinly veiled."

"And so I must be on my best behaviour."

"You are of no consequence Fool. I like you, but you are of no consequence in the games we play. Swords have no friends, merely allies of changing worth. Our lives are eternal contention, and we test the strength of others so that we know our place, and others know their place. My honour is a sign of my strength and my reach, and so I am respected. Or I fail to uphold my honour, and I am bested. I lose face in the eyes of others and become of little consequence.

"There is no road back for a Sword. Honour, once lost, is regained only in a noble death. I tell you these things for my Father and Mother are much influenced by this view, and will look beyond your Fool's garb."

"Thank you for this insight m'Lady."

"My father frets at the life of court. He is a great warrior, mighty in the field, but now my brother minds the daily business of our realm and trains for the day when he will lead our house. By day my father has his dogs, and he hunts and gambles on tourneys and bear-baiting and the like. By night he drinks and picks quarrels, and looks for a woman to bed. You take my meaning?"

"That I might be advised to avoid his gaze and his company?"

"I will do my best to deflect his interest. But you must not encourage it. My Mother defends the honour of my family and her own honour with great energy. She is greatly feared."

"This I have heard."

"My Mother is an academical study in the exercise of power. Her attention, once gained, is a blessing of mixed nature. Best not seek it. She has a discriminating gaze; she finds what she can use and discards what she cannot. And do not imagine that anything goes unseen. Perhaps the only things unseen are the bodies of my Father's paramours."

"You jest m'Lady?"

"It would be wise not to seek for mitigating humour in this situation."

The atmosphere of the court of Swords was not unlike a tavern by the docks, and was, in that respect, familiar. There were more large dogs and the men and women were better looking and better dressed, but the decor was functional, the manners rough, and the humour lewd and loud. Gross insults were common and caused great

KING OF SWORDS

©C.A.L. 2017

laughter; the Fool assumed that, in a culture so prickly, insults were the mark of comrades and close acquaintance.

The Fool saw a difficult audience; rowdy, inattentive, and lewd. After the dinner courses had been served, and the company had settled into heavy drinking, she walked out and began clowning. A few people looked up. On her signal a servant threw a roast chicken in the air and she skewered it with a thrown dagger, then made a clownish show of wrestling it from the dogs and eating as if famished, sharing titbits. There was some laughter. She spun a tankard and made as if draining it to the bottom. Then another, and another, juggling them, but the fourth was full of ale and soaked her as it spun. The court laughed. She mimed anger at the page, and more laughed. Some pages threw balls of straw in the air and she skewered them with knives, one, two, three. There were cheers, and she juggled daggers and then axes to more cheers.

"This Fool," said the King to his wife, "Is a comely wench. And good with a blade."

"Indeed," said the Queen.

The Fool bowed, holding attention at last, and blew a little tune on her whistle. She held out her hand in a gesture of command and dropped it slowly. "Quiet!" voices shouted. And then she sang about Horatius on the bridge, and the hall was still. The only movement was that of wandering dogs. She piped another little tune and sang a song, long forgotten, about a youth who refused to abandon his post on the deck of a burning war galley[2]:

> *Yet beautiful and bright he stood,*
> *As born to rule the storm;*
> *A creature of heroic blood,*
> *A proud though childlike form.*
> *The flames rolled on; he would not go*
> *Without his Father's word;*

---

2   Felicia Dorothea Hemans, *Casabianca.*

172

*That father, faint in death below,*
*His voice no longer heard.*

The hush was tangible. Tears could be seen, even on the cheeks of warriors. Before the applause could begin she sang a melancholy song about a young soldier gone to war, and a mother who waits for news of him:

*Each morn she waited by the door*
*Watching the path from the wood*
*Her lad was gone to a distant war*
*Not knowing if still he stood*
*Or buried deep in a foreign ground*
*Marked by a broken spear*
*She bleeds from an ever-open wound*
*And sheds a grievous tear.*

Now it was time to change the mood, and she began piping popular tunes that all knew, and they began to pour wine and ale and sing with her.

"This is no lacklustre Fool," said the King, "She hath the virtues of a troubadour, the follies of a jester, and the agility of a tumbler."

"Indeed," said the Queen.

A servant came for the Fool. "The Queen desires to see you. Now." Many extravagant tales were told about the Queen of Swords. She was a witch. She was undead. She bathed in the blood of virgins. She kept a giant serpent and it was fed on the children of her enemies. She had the King's amours strangled in their sleep. She knew by heart the genealogy of every great family in the Empire, back to the time when the Sun himself ruled the land during the first Empire of Gold.

Less sensational was the opinion that she was the fine legalist, with an encyclopedic memory for judgement and precedent, and rarely bested in learned debate.

"So Fool, I am told that you travel much and have an agile mind. Tell me something I should know."

"It is not likely that a poor Fool would know anything that might interest you, your Highness."

"If I cease to be interested you will know it quickly."

"The Coins are hiring foreign mercenaries."

"Ah yes, mercenaries. Turncoat cowards selling their loyalty for the afternoon. Brave friends while the sun shines and the ale flows."

"Veterans of foreign wars. These are not raw recruits."

"Old men boasting of their wounds. Good companies are forged in battle, not stamped out at the mint like the silver pennies they are paid. A bold new standard does not a company make. What else?"

"Cups are preaching poverty and denial."

"The Poor Friars?"

"Even the Princess of Cups. The Princess preaches renunciation."

"The *Filii Solis* — I have read it. She encourages the poor to be satisfied with less than they already have. And are we also expected to extol this austerity? I may be persuaded when I see more Cups converted to their own doctrines."

"It is the Staves who rally to the Princess."

"Ah ..."

"There are firebrands among the Staves who speak against wealth and privilege. They declare the equality of all men and women under the Sun, and all wealth to be held in common and used for the common good. They print pamphlets and books calling for revolution."

"So the peasants are revolting. This is not new. They write and print books — this is new, but I am sure we can make a bonfire of these vanities. We will hang a few hotheads."

"The Coins seek to supplant you."

"And how will they achieve that?"

"The potential wealth from trade far exceeds the wealth from land, for the area of land is fixed, but the profit from trade is not."

QUEEN OF SWORDS

©C.A.L. 2017

"Interesting. And how did you learn this?"

"The King of Coins spoke these words to me."

"The King? And how do you interpret them?"

"The nobility owe their wealth to control of the land, and land, however improved, yields only so much income per acre. There are two routes to increased wealth: the first is to acquire more land by conquest, inheritance, or marriage, and the second is to oppress the peasant folk. The Coins owe their wealth to commerce, and the wealth of commerce is in proportion to industry, inventiveness, and freedom to manufacture and trade. It seems to enrich every party, and its wealth has no limit one can easily discern."

"And you imagine a future in which they purchase land and titles and the pretence of nobility, with mercenary armies to do their bidding."

"And a new machinery of war. The Staves have brought inventions from the East. These new inventions require much gold, but they make weapons that strike like the lightning bolts of Jupiter. They declare that men will no longer decide the outcome of battles, that hideous new inventions will strike down whole armies from afar."

"Are you suggesting Swords are obsolete? As if we had not refined the art of warfare? As if we had not invented taxation? Where there is coin, we will have our goodly share."

"The Coins will seek to acquire the means to retain their profits. It is not in their interest to relinquish their principal source of power."

"I see. And so they recruit old soldiers to their cause with golden bounties?"

"Not so old your Highness."

"You did say. Now tell me — and answer frankly — what think you of my children?"

"Your son is mighty on the field, but your daughter may be more fearsome off the field."

"Interesting. Yes, my son has more boyish nobility than this family requires, and my daughter sees the reality of our situation more clearly. Well observed. And how should my daughter marry? A family needs children, and it needs land and good alliances."

"She will resist the notion."

"Indeed she will."

"A scholarly prince, given to study and things of the mind. She will take the reins of power and he will thank her for it."

"Have you such a Prince in mind?"

"The Prince of Staves your Highness."

"What about Cups or Coins? Your view?"

"The Prince of Cups would exasperate with piety. Coins would provide the means to support many ambitions but the tedium of taxes and ledgers would exhaust her patience."

"Interesting. Tell me Mistress Fool ... is it not a burden confining such a mind inside a jester's cap?"

"Being a Fool, I am not burdened with the consequences of my opinions your Highness."

"Indeed. I would be forced to keep you under observation were you wearing any other kind of apparel. Tell me ... are you able to write?"

"Yes your Highness."

"Indeed! Then write me your song of Horatius on the Bridge. I would have it. You may go."

"Thank you your Highness."

ou met Mother?" said the Prince.
"I did m'Lord."

"You seem unscathed."

"I am merely a Fool m'Lord."

"Your Fooling ... it was well done. You are welcome here. Your talent is noised abroad."

"Thank you m'Lord."

# PLAYING THE FOOL

# ᑒ18ᑒ

# THE BONFIRE OF THE VANITIES

*A sanctimonious madness grips the City.*
*The Magician saves his heretical books.*

he Fool returned to the City and it was in an uproar. A
certain level of disorder was customary in the run-up to
the spring equinox. There were processions and festivities
and masques and much lewdness, followed by weeks of
fasting and penance of the sackcloth-and-ashes variety (an economic
necessity for most of the poorer folks, who had been on short rations
since the winter solstice). This year, mobs were jostling through the
streets carrying every manner of luxury: paintings in carved gilt frames,
tapestries, leather-bound books in the finest editions, fashionable clothing, and ancient hand-written scrolls and folios. There was much smoke
and a smell of burning. The Fool spied the Fishwife carrying an armful
of scrolls in the direction of the Great Square.

"What is this tumult and uproar?"

"'Eresy. 'Eresy and sin. We is burnin' sinful pleasures an' works 'o
'eresy and depravity an' intrigues o' the Devil."

"But ... but why?"

"Brother Salvator. Wot 'e preaches. From the pulpit o' San Marco. We must atone fer our sinful ways, atone he sez, atone lest we be's pawns o' the Devil. An' take all thee works o' vanity to the flames. An' these ... these 'ere scrolls are the very Devil's works."

"Let me help you ... you can hasten to fetch some more."

"Thank 'ee Missy Fool, plenty more, plenty more."

The Fool followed the mob to the Great Square, where a fire raged to the height of the tallest guild houses. She spied the Shoemaker looking forlorn, tears streaming down his face.

"An evil day Missy Fool, an evil day," he said, brushing a tear from his cheek. "Tis the smoke, merely the smoke."

"What is this tumult and madness? Our fair city burns its finest."

"The King of Cups has issued a proclamation to renounce sin, the vanities of the flesh, and all the works of the Devil. The Hierophant himself is wearing sackcloth and calls for a renewal of faith. Brother Salvator preaches daily to the mob. This frantic and maddened crowd took my copy of *Shadows of an Unseen World* in the new translation by Marcellus Ficus, printed by the great Manutius. Finest work of Plautus gone in smoke, and I saved for nine Moons to buy it. Tell me you do not share in this fever of destruction?"

"These works I hold I intend to save."

"Then best be quick and best be sly — the mob goes door to door and brooks no resistance."

The Fool found the Magician attempting to conceal books. The task would have been simpler had there been anything other than books to hide the books behind. It had taken the Fool much pleading to gain entrance. The Magician, accustomed to subterfuge, refused to believe the simple proposition that the Fool wanted to enter and had no malicious designs on his books.

"Insanity, insanity, the world has gone mad. The Cups, luxuriating in their wealth and splendour, have a momentary pang of conscience and now I must lose my books. We must prance around in sackcloth and renounce debate, reason, evidence, observation, the entire apparatus of philosophy and the wisdom of untold generations because some sanctimonious mooncalf in a pulpit preaches 'the Devil this' and 'the Devil that' ... if I may speak for the Devil (and as I am oft suspected of heresy perhaps I know his mind with more certainty than our pious Fra. Salvator) then I say the Devil desires a grim and colourless tyranny administered by the narrow in spirit. And as natural hypocrites they still collect their tithes ... lest they hunger for fattened goose after the sanctimonious madness and fasting abates. If ever the Devil cared to play a jest, this would be it."

"In this I concur," the Fool agreed sadly.

"I would stand before my door and let the mob trample me down before they took my books."

"And the mob would be willing to oblige. Have you no plan but some futile concealment?"

"The World has gone awry. Like a top, it falls off its axis and rolls across the floor. When this madness passes they will grieve their loss. Here is the *Yoke and Harness of Necessity* written by Antipodus in the last days of the siege of Syracambis. It is the finest work of natural philosophy ever written. I bought the manuscript from a poor priest I encountered far to the East, translated it myself, and had it printed in two-hundred numbered volumes at my own cost. They would burn it. The mob would dance around the flames, understanding not one word in five, but convinced it preaches diabolical heresy."

"This work sounds most illuminating and a treasure for the wise, but we must deceive and dissemble in haste. The mob comes. Be sly, the Shoemaker said, be sly. Are these not wise words for this occasion? Are we not sly? Is this not Thimblerig writ on a larger canvas?"

"I cannot think! My wits are scattered and in disarray! They fly the field in rout. And here *The Soul of the World*, or in the old tongue, *Anima Mundi*, said to be authored by the most noble Hermes the

Thrice Great, the greatest of all the ancients, for he devised writing, and named the stars. These works are my children. I care for them."

"Can we not conceal them elsewhere? In the Moon Temple? I know the Priestess."

"As do I. But will the mob spare the Moon Temple in their need to find heresies against the Sun?"

"Then where?"

"Who would dare to conceal this manuscript of *The Signatures of Devils and the Doctrine of the Outer Spheres*? Or the *The Book of Zebediah, as Taught Secretly by his Sons James and John*? They are long proscribed in the index of heretical works. Who would be so foolish as to attempt the concealment of these? Were they so foolish, my conscience would rest uneasy, lest they be burned in person before the day was out."

"Then the books remain and we must turn the mob from your door. Sickness — you must physick me."

"They will know it for a deceit, we oft keep company."

"I will divest my Fool's garb and feign affliction. Quick, make the plague mark on the door, and find your crow's mask."

"Yes, the Black Death, this I can do."

With the assistance of chalk and charcoal and red oxide of mercury the Fool was no longer a Fool and bore the terminal marks of the Death. The Fool studied her face in a glass.

"I have traded the face of a Fool for that of a corpse. Whatever place I now have in this world is of limited extent and limited tenure. I must pretend my final hour."

"Even I flinch to witness the extremity writ across your features."

"Burn sulphur. And asafoetida. Let us have an exceeding stink and foulness. I must lie me down, for I tremble and a fierce fever has me in thrall. Aaaargh."

"Let me fire some coals. I will manufacture a most mighty miasma of repellent odour."

And there was the most astonishing effluvium as the Magician ransacked jars and threw the contents onto hot charcoal. After a time coughs, wheezing and red streaming eyes no longer had to be feigned.

"May the mob come soon lest we expire from your stinks and smokes. And while we expire, tell me of *The Yoke and Harness of Necessity*. I have not met Necessity and wish to do so. I have things to say. Harsh things."

"Trip over the lintel and you will meet her face-to-face on the floor. How much harsher an acquaintance do you desire?"

"I am told Necessity is events unfolding as they do because they must, and no power can stay them?"

"Indeed. Events unfold as they must, and so we may study them, assured that if initial circumstances agree, then we will find agreement in outcomes, and all students of causation will concur in observation. Necessity brooks no debate. Necessity bangs her gavel and proclaims the future. My Clockke, if it survives the insanity of our current rampage, is testament to an inflexible cosmic order which it models faithfully. The courses of the Sun and Moon and stars are bound by the statutes of Necessity."

"So why does Urania fret so incessantly at the tardiness of the stars?"

"You jest, surely?"

"And is all of Nature bound so? Is there no domain free of Necessity?"

"Ah, the Great Debate. A student of the great Plautus proposed that the human soul is joined with Necessity, but not governed by her. I have this work here ... by your feet."

A great many books had been concealed beneath the bed-clothes, down the side of the bed, and many more were packed beneath it.

"No no no, let us have no more of books today. Disturb not my bier. A fitting end is it not, the embodiment and articulation of Folly carried to eternal rest upon a bier of Philosophy. I know not whether this be comic or tragic, for Folly, being prodigal, is parent to both. What say you?"

"Tragicomic, a chimera of two dramas sharing one misfortune."

"And would you say philosophy has born much Folly ... in the manner of a bier?"

"I would say Philosophy has bored many Fools."

"Oh, droll. I am fated to expire amongst muscular stenches and limp humour. Bring on the mob I say, for I cannot bier o'er much of this. So ... Necessity ... is the body bound and ruled by Necessity?"

"Clearly so. We fall just as stones do. And it requires the same effort to shift a weight of people as the same weight of stones ... you do recall my *experimentum* with the market porters?" The Magician had paid the porters to ferry people and stones and sacks of turnips and gauge the effort.

"I am certain the porters recall it; they were sorely taxed and much amused."

"But a simple truth was established was it not? That there is no mysterious power in living flesh that triumphs over market porters? We are as stones and turnips? And my *experimentum* with the great beam scale improvised using the Eagle Company's trebuchet? Did that not establish the priority of Necessity over the human soul. Not one person could think themselves lighter. Many tried. Screwed their brows and went red in the face. Necessity triumphed over Will."

"The Baker was not convinced."

"He was waving his arms."

"Is it not said that *soul clap its hands and sing, and louder sing for every tatter in its mortal dress?*"

"He was supposed to sit still. A butterfly flapping its wings would have achieved the same effect on a lesser scale ... had we been using lesser scales. That gormless flapping was not soul o'erpowering Necessity. Whatever power of influence soul possesses, it has been beyond my ability to detect."

"So how does soul enter this world if Necessity watches the gate?"

"Through a sally-port it would seem. You should talk to the High Priestess. She has a disparaging view of Necessity."

"Is that so?"

"It is."

There was a pounding at the door. "Open, lest we break thee hinges!" The Magician adjusted his crow's mask and went to open the door.

MAGICIAN: "See you not the mark? Here! On the door post. The plague mark?"

MOB LEADER: "We seek the artifice of Vanity and of Sin. Stand aside!"

MAGICIAN: "All you will find here is Death, enough for all, and more besides. A pilgrim new arrived from Velzna bears the marks of the Black Death."

MOB LEADER: "What foulness (cough) ... what ill is here?"

FOOL: "Aaaargh"

MANY: "Tis an *ill* smell." "What affliction is this." "Tis the Death, I done seen it!" "Turn aside I say!"

FOOL: "Aaaargh"

MANY: "Turn back!" "Tis the Death!" "The mark, the plague mark!" "The Death!"

MAGICIAN: "The Death is here! Flee this place!"

The Magician bolted the door and removed the beaked mask of a plague doctor.

"That was easily accomplished."

"Aaaargh"

"You are done with Death, although you must subsist upon Philosophy."

"Death is an easy role and one we must all play. And philosophy makes for a lumpy bed."

"And are you also done with playing the Fool?"

185

"I like the role. It suits me well."

"We are confined. The plague mark is upon the door. You are released from Fooling."

"But not from decency. I must be garbed as a Fool once again, although I will humour you and dispense with my cap. You can teach me the devious art of Thimblerig, and I will teach you to sing, and we will soon grow to hate this confinement. And each other."

# ❧19❧

# ON VIRTUE

*In which the Fool is troubled by introspection and consults the Virtues for advice.*

*"Whence things have their origin,*
*Thence also their destruction happens,*
*According to Necessity;*
*For they give to each other Justice and recompense*
*For their Injustice*
*In conformity with the ordinance of Time."*
*Anaximander*

fter many days of confinement with the Magician the Fool had an irresistible desire for fresh mountain air. During her confinement she had been seized by a terrible melancholy that she could not shake.

"I no longer feel myself," said the Fool to the Hermit.

"And why is that?"

"I desired to impress the Queen of Swords."

"I cannot fault the magnitude of your ambition. Was this to be your masterpiece of Folly?"

"So it would seem to be. I told her the Staves were printing books calling for revolution. *She* said the Swords would make a bonfire of those vanities. Fra. Salvatore called for a bonfire of the vanities from the *pulpitum* of San Marco. *Then* the city was in an uproar, and Cups and their followers were preaching the vanity of knowledge and burning books, and all was madness."

"And you believe you might be to blame?"

"There is a coincidence of themes is there not? And in time?"

"I do not see that. The Cups have been in turmoil and dispute for tens of years. Of that entire community, half of the Cups are passionate to defend the minutiae of their sacred traditions to the death; another quarter believe in the primacy of individual revelation such as the Princess preaches, and the remaining quarter — now that printers are printing the sacred texts in the common speech — the remaining quarter are asserting that they no longer require priests or temples, and all traditions are corrupt, as evidenced by new vernacular readings of the scriptures."

"Then you do not believe I am to blame?"

"I do not. There were bonfires of vanities when I was a young man. In my day as Emperor there were great multitudes of penitents flogging themselves and each other till blood ran in streams and filled the cobbles. There were purges of heretics. There are maladies of the mind that sweep through the City every few decades, just as do the black fever and the bloody flux."

"You are kind. But yet I am confounded. I was proud of Folly. Now it seems that I am nought but an addlepate."

"That is a most ungenerous thought."

"In my melancholy it seems to me that my pride in Folly was overweening self-regard. I believed myself free and unfettered, and superior to any fixed station in life. And now I am confounded."

"What occasioned this fall into self-examination and bitter self-regard?"

"I met the Swords. You know them better than do I. They are fierce and barbarous and think themselves superior ... but their self-regard resembles a strong tower stationed on a tall hill. They have a strength. They have measured themselves, and so they measure others. In my folly I wanted not to be a Fool and to be measured and found

VIII Strength

©C.A.L 2017

worthy."

"And are you worthy?"

"I am confounded."

"You have begun to measure yourself. As they do."

"Yes."

"You see yourself as another does. This brings discomfort."

"If I could return to Folly. I am provoked by myself. I am affronted by what was hidden from me. I do not desire this double vision — if only I could hide from myself, ducking behind the trunk of a tree as does the crafty squirrel."

"You recoil from yourself? It requires Strength to bear the sight of oneself. But take heart, your natural disposition will return. It requires stamina to sustain this passion of disdain. Recall that Strength has closed the mouth of the Lion and now they are amicable. These feelings are like mist and will pass. You will Fool again."

"But I will not be the same. I will be doubled and witness myself as I am Fooling."

"You have become separate within yourself. You would return to being an innocent child playing in the Sun?"

"Most certainly! And no!"

"Your soul is divided. You cannot unsee and so you are obliged move forward and endure the sight of yourself. You will witness the irreducible folly of this world in your own particularity. It is what philosophers call 'ignorance'. You may be repulsed by what you see in yourself. If you endure, you will rediscover your innocence."

"You know of this? You have found it in your books?"

"I have. It is an affliction of the philosophical mind. Here is one example, *The Dialogues of Plautus*. A gaggle of ancient folks stand in a market and discuss the human condition. So, for example, they try to decide what is Good."

"And do they find out?"

"No, but I enjoy the subtlety of argument. You have the singular advantage of being able to talk to the Virtues directly, so in your case I would think the argument superfluous."

"You suggest that I talk to the Virtues?"

"As I recall you have talked with them many times, especially Temperance. I was thinking there might be an additional benefit to be gained from listening to them."

"You wound me! It is said that when the spleen is afflicted, black bile poisons the blood and makes one bitter and uncharitable."

"Merely observant my dear. I am too old for lies and too old for malice."

"In that case I am going to talk to Justice. I have a bone to pick."

There is no Justice in the world!"

"It would assist me if you were less passionate in your declarations and more specific," Justice replied defensively.

"The Empire is run by vile people who do vile things to almost everyone. They tax the poor until they starve, they force the homeless into slave labour, they hang poor boys for having opinions, and the Emperor's favourite General burns our villages to provide a deniable *causus belli*. The Coins force decent farmers off land they have farmed for generations because they are unable to pay exorbitant tithes demanded by the Coins in the first place. Everywhere I go most people are suffering and a small number of people are the cause of it. So where is Justice?"

"Is this a general question or a personal attack?"

"I am out of temper, I did not intend to be disagreeable."

"I will ask you a question. If you have a puppy and you beat it whenever it is disobedient, what does it learn?"

"It learns to be afraid."

"So punishment alone is not Justice. And if we punish a child for snatching a toy, or hitting another child, or stealing from the market, as most children do at some point. What is the lesson?"

"To become devious and so avoid punishment."

"And what other lesson might we teach?"

"Explain to the child how the offended party feels."

"Quite. You expound the essential nature of Justice, that one must consider the rights and feelings of others, and give them equal weight to one's own."

"The Prince of Cups preaches this each year in his midsummer solstice sermon."

"Quite so. The Cups are an integral part of my outreach programme."

"So you do not punish evil people?"

"I see my role as education."

"But what of those who are indifferent to the feelings of others? They lie and cheat and steal and murder, and employ all manner of brutal means to become our masters, and then make laws to subdue us. I cite the General, who has all the honours the Empire can bestow and yet respects nothing. And the King of Coins. Why is there no Justice? Can you not petition Jupiter to employ his thunderbolts? That would deal with the General most effectively."

"The General uses subordinates to avoid culpability. Would you have Jupiter roast farm boys for acting under orders?"

"I am weary of these studied examples. Always there are hypotheticals to obstruct me. What if the General is caring for a child ... so we must spare him. What if he is loved by his aged mother? How the General's dog might mourn his untimely passing. He is much encouraged by those of a military bent, indeed, he is a victim of a culture of violence. No! The General is evil. When there are extremes there is no need to debate the nuances. Big lightning! Flash! Bang! The world is a better place."

"Your talent is better adapted to the theatre than the tribunal."

"You have that magnificent sword! And that golden balance! And a most excellent gown of great worth. It seems you are also arrayed for

XI JUSTICE

©C. A. L. 2017

theatre!"

Justice looked peeved. "You fail to comprehend the full significance of free-will. One cannot go about blasting people whenever they offend you. That would be tyranny. It is unfair to find fault with Justice when there are pathologies of free-will that were not anticipated."

"Such as?"

"The Devil."

"You did not anticipate the Devil? Like ... duh!"

"The Sun did not anticipate how influential the Devil's existential position would be. The Sun loves all beings and has no malice."

"So what is to be done?"

"You seek to remedy the world?"

"Yes! I seek to remedy the world."

"Then you must first remove free will. Remove free will and the Devil will be snuffed out. And also your Folly. You will be confined to a narrow track and there will be no more roaming around the country-side, or quarrelsome questions and disputations, or singing 'The Bear with no Hair' at an offensive volume in the small hours of the morning."

"Then let us retain free will and explore other means. Will evil doers be punished after death? The Hierophant says that the wicked will be judged and plunged in a lake of fire. I would love to see this lake."

"I do not have a lake of fire."

"Really. No lake of fire?"

"We discussed it, and the Sun, who is without malice, would not countenance the idea."

"I am sure the Devil would love a lake of fire. He likes throwing people into swamps, and fire could only increase his entertainment."

"I am certain he would, but there is no lake. There are no pools of boiling pitch, or devils equipped with flays and hooks. It would seem your Hierophant has taken more inspiration from the Devil than the

194

Sun he professes to serve."

"That is going to make a lot of people unhappy."

"I expect it will. The Sun wants to keep his options open. The issue under debate is how we process the Devil and all evil-doers. We cannot extinguish them, for they have divine souls. Should we make another cosmos of pure evil for them to inhabit, like a large gaol? Or should we leave them here in this world to complete its ruination and take all the goodly people out to a new and better world? A brave new world in which free-will is tempered by a demonstrated Virtue. Personally, I am in favour of remediation and rehabilitation. Even the most evil people have a spark of the Sun in them, a sunbeam trying to shine."

"You are most solicitous ..."

" We have considered returning each soul to the world many times in all forms and conditions so that souls might learn the true meaning of Justice. We have run projections and we estimate it will take five billion lifetimes to clean up the existing mess and move everyone to an acceptable level of self-realisation."

"You have run projections?"

"We have some very capable angels on the team. Look, I am sensing hostility."

"No, no, I am content. I just thought ... no, it's fine."

he Fool returned to the Hermit. "I talked to Justice."

"And?"

"Evil is a complex matter and Justice an intractable mess."

"You thought Justice should be more tangible and direct."

"That is an elegant way of putting it. I wish I had said that."

"I think Justice sees her role as promoting the ideals of Justice. Let me tell you a story.

"On the first day of creation, the Sun assembled the Moon and the Star and the Devil and all the angels and explained what He had in mind. The Sun said 'I want you to meet Necessity. Necessity is going to run the world.' Necessity explained how beautifully organised and ordered the Cosmos was going to be. The Cosmos was going to be a work of elegance and refined beauty, in which all aspects were perfectly harmonised. The Devil was horrified by this idea, and suggested the cosmos should be run by Chaos, and Chaos explained the value of openness and emergence and novelty. The Sun, being the Sun, could see the value in both arguments, and decided to compromise. Substance, which is the child of Necessity, would constitute the bulk of the Cosmos. However, each living thing would contain a spark of the Sun, and that spark would have the nature of Freedom (and Freedom is the Sun's name for what the Devil calls Chaos). Like all compromises, this made everyone unhappy."

The Fool frowned. "So the soul is ruled by both by the Sun and the Devil, and what the Sun calls Freedom the Devil calls Chaos, and they are the same thing?"

"Freedom is the residue that remains when Chaos has been subdued by Necessity ... but yes, that would seem to be the lesson in the story. The story continues ... Necessity refused to administer the Cosmos if living beings were going to be influenced by Chaos. 'It will be an incontinent mess and I am not going to take the blame,' she said. The Sun tried to appease her by appointing four Virtues to advise the soul, that the soul might be guided away from the more disruptive aspects of Chaos."

"To *advise* the soul?"

"Yes."

"So the Sun let the Devil have his way, and came up with an asinine solution to try to appease Necessity?"

"You can understand why this story is not widely told."

"How did you find out about this? Are you really Prudence? Were you there when the Sun made the Cosmos?"

"Ah ... no. Prudence is an honorary position. It is awarded to those who are old and have lived wisely. The other Virtues embody principles, whereas Prudence embodies experience, and the wisdom that comes from making mistakes."

"So I could be Prudence? I have made so many mistakes."

"Once you have abandoned Folly I believe you would make an admirable Prudence."

"Do I need to make many more mistakes, or have I made sufficient?"

"I believe you will make many more mistakes before you are done with Folly."

"I could go and make some more right now? Would that help?"

"I think you have misunderstood the nature of Prudence."

# Playing the Fool

# ❧20❧

# Running with the Moon

*The Fool, much perplexed by Necessity, seeks out the Moon.*
*There is much running. And dancing. And keeping up.*

Quand nul ne la regarde
La mer n'est plus la mer,
Elle est ce que nous sommes
Lorsque nul ne nous voit.
Elle a d'autres poissons,
D'autres vagues aussi.
C'est la mer pour la mer
Et pour ceux qui en rêvent
Comme je fais ici.

La Mer Secrète, Jules Supervielle

he Fool visited the High Priestess in her temple. She want-
ed to talk about Necessity.
"Good morn to you Miranda."
"Shhh!"
"Is this still a secret? Now that you are no longer a Fool?"
"Yes. I think so. Yes. And I am still a Fool."
"As you wish. And how may I assist?"
"The World is much afflicted by Necessity."
"Things as they must be? The Great Wheel?"
"A Wheel? Necessity resembles a Wheel?"

199

"The Sun and Moon and stars go around and around. Each day seems new and fresh, and yet stones still fall, fire burns, water does not flow uphill, the wind brings hot or cold according to season. There is unceasing movement that goes around and transports us from day to day, but it conceals an axis of truth that does not change. Motion and stillness. A wheel. Necessity is a wheel."

"A wheel, but not like Fortune?"

"Fortune is individual destiny for better or worse. Lucky people are chosen by the Lady Fortuna. They rise to the peak of the Wheel, where they marvel at their luck or brag of their talent, and then they fall. Whatever their fortune, whether it is good or bad ... old age, weakness and death awaits them. Death claims them all. The Lady Fortuna may have her favourites, but Necessity is like the mill wheel that grinds small and spares none."

"It seems to me that Necessity is the source of much evil."

"How so?"

"Every creature that lives must eat and drink and sleep and must do so at the expense of others. Rabbits eat grass, foxes hunt rabbits, men hunt foxes, and men kill other men, and all so that they might live. Every animal that has ever lived has been killed and eaten, or has found a lonely place to die. The Empress, who is kind and gentle, would still protect her own. Necessity is cruel, and she makes us cruel to each other. It is said that Necessity is beautiful and dances naked behind the veil of substance, but I cannot help but see her as a grim queen on an iron throne."

"The Sun struck an unpalatable bargain."

"You blame the Sun?"

"I do. The Moon would not countenance such an agreement."

"But why?"

"The Sun chose a world in which past, present and future rest on a stable foundation. The Moon chose a world in which the present is loosely attached to past and future and is mutable in ways this world of Necessity is not. The Moon is mutable and the Sun is steady, that is their natures. In the beginning the Sun interviewed both Necessity and Dream, and chose Necessity."

"And the Moon chose Dream?"

"Yes."

"And does the Moon have a world just as the Sun does?"

"She does. She has a world. But if Necessity is like the firm, dry land, then the world of the Moon is like the sea — ever-shifting, perilous, and secretive."

"I would witness it."

"You are mortal, a child of Necessity. The world of the Moon might birth in you another kind of Folly, and not the sweet kind. You will have seen this? When wits are disordered and the dictates of Necessity are ignored?"

"A mooncalf?"

"Children of the Moon. Mooncalves. Lunatics. A hurtful manner of speech."

"I would witness the Moon's world in any case. As a Fool I should master my vocation."

"I thought you might. So come."

The High Priestess led the Fool through basement levels of the Temple and then down a stone stair that seemed interminable. The stone grew hoary and damp.

"Cities grow upwards, did you know that? With each passing century the ground becomes higher and the past lower. What was once in the daylight is buried deep, and a roof becomes a floor, and then a cellar, and then a forgotten tile in the earth. There is much in the City lost beneath two-score cubits of dust and night soil and ash and broken things. Tombs, temples, cellars, even palaces whole and entire, sunk far beyond sight and falling into ruin."

"And this is your past?"

"This was once the present of the first Priestess who ordered it

XVIII THE MOON

©C.A.L. 2017

made. Here, the Gateway of the Moon."

A circular room of ancient black stone contained a mirror of polished black stone four cubits high. The priestess lit oil lamps.

"It is a mirror but it is also a gate."

"It seems somewhat solid for a gate."

"We employ this for our journey." The Priestess held out a small jar. "Then the Gate seems not so solid."

"A salve?"

"Rub a little on the inside of your elbows, under your arms, on the inside of your thighs, behind your knees, and under your chin."

And after several minutes: "My heart pounds, I sweat, and yet I am chilled and shaking."

"Wrap yourself in this robe. I will watch over you. Now regard your reflection."

"I feel most strange."

"I will sing the Moon song for you. The Moon will appear in the mirror and you will step through."

Excuse me, your most luminous magnificence," said the Fool to the Moon.

"Oh, Miranda! You alarmed me. I did not discern your approach."

"I came through the Moon Gate."

"Then you wish to join me tonight?"

"If you will permit me."

"I do, but you will have to keep up. The pace is swift."

"You seem so different ... so athletic."

"I am different on each and every night. Greet my hounds that they know you, for tonight is the Wild Hunt from dusk until dawn, and you will need to keep up."

"I know all the paths."

"Do you indeed? We will see. Come, prepare yourself. Come Lux, come Tenebra, to me, to me!"

And so they ran. The woods were wild and dark, and the silver figure of the Moon, bow in hand and flanked by her two great hounds, slipped lightly through tangle and thicket. The bow of the sickle Moon above cast a silvery light on leaf and web, and the glossy leaves of ivy shone like mirrors on the trunks of trees.

"You are there in the sky and yet you are here also," panted the Fool.

"I am not bound by Necessity. I am not fastened to place or time as you are. I am everywhere I want to be. Now run, run, for the Hunt begins."

It seemed to the Fool that a myriad of silver beings ran alongside, flowing through the trees like quicksilver, and in the distance a silver stag leapt and bounded just out of bow shot. Then, without leaving the tangles of the dark wood, they were also in the sky, and the stag darted left and right through banks of cloud. And they were in the sea in pursuit of a great silver fish (or something, it was silver), and Tritons blew conch shells and hurled tridents, and in water, on earth, and in the sky the whole of creation seemed to be in pursuit of the unattainable, every star and spark and mote of being in a tumultuous quest. And the Moon cried "Keep up, keep up, there is far to go!"

And then, in a manner that the Fool could neither recall or comprehend, there was a wild celebration in a clearing. The Fool was much changed and danced naked on strange legs, playing wild ecstatic tunes on her elderwood whistle. Many wild things danced and pranced and bucked and leapt in a mindless joy, and the Moon danced with them, her silver bow trailing silver light in the air. There were goat people, and rabbit people, and fox people, and deer people, and wolf people, and bear people, and everything that was wild and could know joy, *was wild*, and *knew joy*, and all were one in the dance. And yet ... she was flying in the sky and running in the forest and swimming in the sea, and the hunt and the dance and the wild music were somehow the same and somehow different.

Then there was no Fool because she was in too many places and in too many beings. The Fool had been a little more than a skein of memory woven by the loom and shuttle of space and time. The thread had broken. Necessity made a despairing gesture and backed out of the room. Dream walked in, and smiled a patronising smile.

"Miranda!" The High Priestess was shaking her gently in the ancient chamber far beneath the city. "Drink this."

She drank, and they were quiet for a time.

"Hast thee some semblance of wits remaining?"

"I think so."

"You met the Moon? And talked about Necessity?"

"We chased and danced. There was little conversation beyond 'Keep up! Keep up!'"

"Are you satisfied?"

"I am."

Were you able to confer about Necessity?" asked the Magician.

"Not so much talk," said the Fool. "I hunted with the Moon."

"And what did you learn?"

"Necessity ... straightens things out and makes them real. And it makes us real too. Real to ourselves."

"Know thyself ... is that your meaning?"

"I am entirely a creature of Necessity. I did not know that. Now I do."

"Perhaps not entirely. It seems to me that Folly lies beyond the straight confine of Necessity. You must tell me more."

"I am perplexed," she said, "my wits are not yet ready to spin out the tale. They are bewildered. The Moon weaves a greater Folly than I had conceived of — I have witnessed a Folly writ larger than the World."

# Playing the Fool

# ❧21❧

# DEATH

*In which our Fool is not a Fool.*

he Fool was deeply asleep by a sputtering camp-fire in the woods when she heard a roar and woke with a start. Strength and the Lion were standing over her. The fire had burned down, and yet the clearing was filled with a strange light.

"You must come to the mountains. The Hermit sends for you."

"The Hermit? My feet are sore weary from travel and the City is but a day from here, and there I can rest. The mountains are many days from here."

"He sends for you. You must come without delay. Come, ride on the Lion's back. Let us away!"

And so the Fool gathered her few possessions in that eerie light and cautiously mounted the Lion's back, holding tight to his fur. She could not tell how they travelled, or whether she slept, but soon they were in the mountains and it was daylight and they ran together up the rocky path to the Hermit's cave.

"He is here, come inside," said Strength, holding back a faded covering that served as a door to the cave. Inside the Fool could only just distinguish Temperance and Justice, and in a corner, Death was sitting on a stool. The Hermit was lying on the rough pallet that served as a bed, his head propped on a bearskin that was serving as a pillow.

"Shhh," said Strength, "he sleeps. He will be pleased that you are here. Come ..." She took the Fool by the arm and led her back outside. "For many Moons he has complained of feeling sick after eating. Now he cannot stand and does not eat. We give him a little broth."

"We must return to the City in haste and fetch the Magician. He will physick to him ..."

"Did you not see Death? Sitting on the stool? He came yesterday and spoke to the Hermit, and so we came to fetch you."

"But the Hermit often converses with Death."

"This is different."

The Hermit woke and the Fool sat down by the bed.

"Miranda, you came!"

"You know my name!"

"Of course I do."

"I did not tell it."

"You did not have to. Tell me what new adventures you have had."

"I hunted with the Moon."

"O, most excellent. Some nights I feel sure I can hear the cries and tumult of the Hunt. And did you dance?"

"I danced. I played my little whistle and it seemed that all the company of the Moon were one with my tune."

"Play for me now. Play the tune that even the Moon danced to."

The Fool played a tune, although she could not swear that it was the same tune, but it was merry and even the Virtues seemed less solemn.

"How do you feel?"

208

"Most weak ... but I have Strength as a nurse and she supports me ... it is most damnable that so little goes into my mouth but so much still leaves this old bag of bones."

He was a bag of bones. His skin was like the finest parchment when it has dried too long, fragile and transparent and prone to tearing. His face, once so cheery, had collapsed onto his skull, the skin hanging and infinitely wrinkled.

"You won't die. I will send the Virtues off to the markets for fresh food and we will make a better broth, and I will keep Death busy counting all stars in the sky or some such nonsense, and we will have you well again."

"I have spoken with Death. We are in agreement."

"But I don't agree!"

There was a long silence, and the Fool wept bitterly. After a time the Hermit slept, and the Fool confronted Death.

"You can't take him! He's a good man. There are so many evil men. Leave him. Go away ..." But Death sat on the stool and said nothing. Death looked at the Fool with eyes so filled with pity and grief she began to weep again.

After a time Strength held her. "You cannot change this," she said.

"Have some wine," said Temperance, "you are weary."

The Hermit was too weak to use his arms and legs to move himself. Two or three times an hour the Fool asked if he was comfortable, and they devised ways to turn him over gently, and prop him on one side or another. He could talk, but the effort was great. He preferred to communicate with an imperceptible nod or shake of his head. Sometimes he needed to go outside for his toilet, and Strength would pick him up.

"This is horrible," she said after the skin on his arm tore. "I cannot use my strength without hurting him. We must find a better way." They experimented with animal skins and poles and tried to roll him onto a stretcher, but that was no better.

"If he fouls himself I will clean him," said the Fool, and she did. It broke her heart to see a proud man reduced to such indignity. Sometimes the light came back into his eyes and they talked.

"Why is Death being so monstrous?" asked the Fool. "He just sits there and watches."

"My time has not yet run out," said the Hermit.

"I don't want you to go," said the Fool. "Tell him to go away. I was not frightened by Death, but now I fear him terribly."

"Look at the entrance," said the Hermit, "What do you see?"

"Outside."

"How do you see it?"

"Small."

Justice stepped forward. "All the cares and concerns of the world seem far away to him. Even before this sickness he was ready."

"Age ... diminishes ... the world," said the Hermit. "I have something to tell you Miranda. Alone. Strength ... shoosh them all out ... even Death."

The Virtues left the cave, and the Lion glared at Death from such a short distance that he left also. The Hermit told the Fool something that could not be heard, and she hugged him close and cried for a very long time.

For two weeks little changed. The Hermit shrank and no longer resembled a living being. The Fool lay on the floor by the bed and slept when she could. If his breathing altered she sat up and counted the breaths, and thought that his time had come. She held his hand so that he knew she was still with him. He did not die.

In the third week the Fool began to berate Death. She was angry and said vile things to the figure on the stool. She grabbed the stool from under Death and threw it out of the cave, and Temperance brought it back and gave the Fool a stern look. The Hermit could no

XIII DEATH

©C.A.L. 2017

longer talk, and blinked his eyes in response to a question. He could no longer swallow and could take no broth. The Fool stood at the entrance to the cave, so far beyond tiredness and pain and grief that she was utterly dead inside and said:

"He must die now. He must."

Strength held her tight and said "Be strong."

Still he did not die. The Fool grovelled on the floor and implored Death to take him, but Death sat and regarded her with a measureless pity. The Hermit was no longer conscious and his breathing grew laboured and heavy, and still he did not die. She held his hand throughout the night, and still he breathed, and finally she slept. Strength covered her with her cloak. For two more infinitely long days she sat by the bed, and he did not die.

"Go and take some air," said Strength, "I will watch."

"He is so close," said the Fool. "I must not leave."

"I will call you," said Strength.

The Fool went outside. The world had shrunk. The wind was clean and fresh, but there was no reality beyond the breathing of the man on the bed in the cave. She had entered the Kingdom of Death, and was powerless to leave.

The Fool spent another night by his bedside, and as dawn broke and light filtered into the cave, the intervals between each breath grew longer. Death rose from his place on the stool and came over to the bed. There was a last breath, and the Hermit was gone. The Fool waited and waited, but now that Death had come she could see the Folly in all the previous moments. He was dead. There would be no more breaths. She turned to thank Death, relieved that the end had finally come, but the cave was empty. She was alone. She sat with the body for hours and wept.

group came from the nearest village bearing flowers and small gifts of food and drink.

"He came to us in dream. We knew he was gone."

Two of the women helped the Fool prepare the body, and some men went off to prepare the place of the dead. The earth was sparse and shallow, and bodies were left in a nearby valley for the vultures that soared among the highest peaks. Many more villagers came from a score of miles, and when they carried him to the place of the dead, there were perhaps a hundred who stood and listened to the words that were said.

The Fool returned to the empty cave. She felt an uncanny sense of violation in being there alone, with only his books and some simple possessions. She went through the books and discovered a folio, hand-written and roughly bound. In it was an inscription:

"To Miranda, that you may embrace Virtue."

She settled down to read. Some villagers brought bowls of food, and she bowed to them and thanked them, and ate.

After some reading she thought: "It seems to me that Folly and Virtue are opposed, for the Fool is easily swayed, impulsive, and blind to consequence, while Virtue looks ahead and seeks a wholesome path for the benefit of many. The Hermit writes that the soul seeks to grow beyond its confines just as the serpent sloughs its skin. Virtue is not the business of polishing one's soul as the Devil asserts ... it is a matter of respecting a larger world and diminishing one's arrogance in relation to others. A voice in my soul agrees. And yet I am divided and the Fool in me longs for the Devil and his tunes. There is comfort in being small and of no consequence, and yet an angel whispers 'Grow! Grow!'. Perhaps I can practice Virtue and pretend to be a Fool?"

"Perhaps we can help?" said Temperance.

"You have returned?"

"Would you like some wine?" said Temperance.

"I have missed you. You are much kinder than I thought you would be. All of you."

"Will you remain here?" asked Justice. "The villagers like you.

213

They believe you are touched by a good spirit."

"I will stay some days and read the words of the Hermit. I have much to think about. You are welcome to keep me company."

"Do you cast off the mantle of a Fool," asked Strength. "Change requires strength and courage. And you will require strength and courage to view the world's Folly without flinching."

"I will retain this motley garb and cap of a Fool ... but I will also measure myself to see whether Virtue might fit me and be snug."

# ᔯ22ᔰ

# MEETING THE STAVES

*"The instrument of labour, when it takes the form of a machine,*
*immediately becomes a competitor of the workman himself."*
Karl Marx

t was an item of belief among the Staves that they did everything of consequence. They grew food, built cities, cut timber, smelted steel, worked the mills, and raised the horses, donkeys, mules and oxen that provided the essential motive power for the Empire.

Staves could be prickly and pugnacious. They saw some value in Cups, who were decent folks for the most part. They regarded Swords as rapacious thugs who took more pleasure in destruction than in building (and there was nothing a Stave disliked more than seeing a good thing destroyed). The Coins were parasites who drained off most of their money, stole their land, and in return provided them with 'jobs'.

In turn the Swords and Coins feared the energy and inventiveness of the Staves and conspired together to render them divided and powerless. More than any external enemy, they feared an army of Staves raised in revolt.

The Fool, being the least practical of people, loved the homely competence of the Staves, but feared their judgements. You don't know

215

how to milk a goat? Make butter and cheese? Spin wool? Weave? Don't know the Moons for planting turnips? Barley? Oats? Peas? Don't understand the intricacy of irrigation channels with their myriad gates and sluices? Don't know how to turn the leg of a chair on a lathe? Sharpen a chisel? Hammer an ingot of steel into shearing shears? Don't know how to lay a foundation? Thatch a roof? Carve an ornamental lintel? Tell a mason from his mark?

The Staves were fierce and proud and wore old grubby clothes as they went about their business. They were comfortable with dirt. They made a mess, and they tidied it away. On the day of the Sun they came together in their best clothes, all washed and clean. They stood in the temples and praised the Sun. They were disciplined, fastidious, and intolerant, ate heartily, drank too much, and died too young.

Staves had discovered how to make paper and the moveable-type printing press (it was said their Princess had discovered the secrets far to the East). This miraculous new invention was the cause of a storm of handbills that were nailed to doors, pasted to walls, and passed about in secret. These handbills were scurrilous, inflammatory, hilarious, and scandalous. They parodied the royalty of Coins and Swords, portrayed lewd sexual acts, and called for revolution.

Printers were the most belligerent of the Staves. Self-educated and literate, they were infinitely quarrelsome, quick to take issue, self-organising ... and just as rapidly, splitting apart in acrimony. In a single generation they had taken from the Cups the task of preserving knowledge and were determined that all should read and own books and become as opinionated and idiosyncratic as they were themselves. Although it was difficult to identify any shared opinion among printers, there was a pervasive belief in an intellectual equality in which all opinion and knowledge should be freely shared and debated in public. Some thought that if knowledge was a common inheritance, then the same principles should apply to land and to property.

The Fool lived a life free of practical wisdom, and free of the accompanying dirt, sweat and tedium that was part of any encounter with the necessities of the world. The Fool enjoyed her freedom from daily toil. The Staves wanted freedom, but it was a more difficult and dangerous freedom they called for in their handbills. When she had comprehended the perilous and dangerous path to freedom that some firebrands were calling out for, she understood her naivety. She could be free because she did not matter, she was superfluous. The Staves were not superfluous.

"Practical wisdom," the Hermit had said, "they know how to do things. Important and useful things. You are kind and funny, but in truth humour is best appreciated in front of a warm fire and after a good meal. Someone has to know how to forge and sharpen an axe. Some-one has to chop wood, or winters would be even colder than they are. Someone has to tend the land and grow food, or wastrels like thee and me would starve."

The Princess of Staves was a great traveller. "We cannot afford to be narrow in outlook," she is recalled as saying. "The world is a ferment of ingenuity and invention; everywhere there are new discover-ies and new ways of doing new things. We can learn much from other peoples. We cannot afford to sit at home and do the same old things in the same old way."

Inevitably a voice would pipe up: "And what be wrong with that? Traditional ways are tried and tested."

"Because we will be replaced," she would reply. "In the best case we will be replaced by our children, who will learn new ways and better skills. In the worst case, by those in other climes, and our silver will go to other people who do not shirk innovation. The aged cling to old ways even when new ways are better."

"That's not a fair comparison Missy Princess, not fair at all. Us old folks can do a job in half the time that a youngster can, and have the experience of tools and materials. You can't replace that; every job is different."

PRINCESS OF STAVES

©C.A.L. 2017

"We will be replaced," insisted the Princess. "Better tools, better methods, better materials. Today I witnessed a marvellous new plough and harness, it sweeps through the soil like a brave ship under full sail. And look what happened to the Cups. I still hear elderly monks talking about how wonderful it was to copy a manuscript by hand — the sense of peace, the communion with Spirit. And in a lifetime they would copy how many books? A dozen? Two dozen? But now who wants to pay for a monk to copy a book when one can print hundreds and thousands."

"But beggin' yer pardon Missy Princess, their books are things of beauty."

And that is how it was with the Staves: opinionated, often quarrelsome, never loathe to argue a point. The Princess was passionate about invention. Improved windmills, waterwheels, the design of ploughshares, the storage of food ("do you know how much is wasted?"), dams and irrigation, crop varieties, reaping and threshing, animal husbandry, crop rotation, instruments of navigation, shipbuilding.

And the production of cloth. Like all young women of status she had been required to master the finer arts of spinning, weaving and embroidery. Her peers spent their lives creating wall hangings showing *The Surrender of the Illyrians*, and other noble and inspiring images. Being of an active temperament, she resented every moment spent with a loom or needle, and spent the hours of enforced tedium devising elaborate machines for the production of cloth.

"Why should I make one tapestry if I can discover how to make a thousand tapestries with no more effort. Like printing, but in cloth. Every home would be like a castle; every woman would dress like a queen."

The Fool met the Princess in a tavern. The Princess had returned to the City after two years of travel to a far-off land (rumoured to be somewhere to the East). It was late afternoon on the day of the

Sun and they were all drunk and rowdy. The Princess reached into her satchel and pulled out a small horn with an ornate brass lid and unusual decoration. She poured some black powder on the bench and struck a spark over it using a flint. There was a stupendous flash and a dense cloud of choking smoke rose to the ceiling. Drinks were knocked over, chairs overturned, and cats and dogs dashed to safety.

"I brought this from a far-off land," the Princess announced dramatically. "In the land of Khitai they call it 'The Powder that Destroys Earth and Illuminates Heaven'".

"Sun's teeth!" thought the Fool to herself. "The Magician will want some of that."

"And I brought this," the Princess announced, now that she had the undivided attention of the room. It was a piece of cloth that flowed through her fingers almost like a liquid. "They make it from this," and she held up a white bobbin.

"I know what 'at be!" a voice piped-up. "I finds 'em feedin' on me mulberry trees."

"Barkeep," said the Princess, "Pour that man another ale."

Later, as the tavern emptied and patrons retired to bed, and the Fool had earned her keep juggling bowls and tankards, she found an opportunity to talk to the Princess.

"I am told you are something of a traveller," said the Princess.

"I have been to the very ends of the Earth!" said the Fool dramatically.

"Very droll. Of course, every sailor of competence knows that the world is round. Why else do ships fall below the horizon in proportion to their distance? And as one climbs a mast, they are revealed once again. It is trivial geometry to calculate the circumference. I expect you speak figuratively?"

"No, literally. There are four great Towers that bound space and sustain existence."

220

"How amusing, my nurse told me this. And angels?"

"Yes, they are garrisoned by angels, but the angels have no souls and are ordained to act always as they were originally created."

"Like automata?"

"Yes."

"How marvellous. If only we had a weaving automaton ... we could undercut the Illyrians. I have wasted many hours on this. Next time you go to the ends of the Earth, bring me back the secrets of automata. You will find me most generous."

"It would seem to be a simple matter your Highness. The angels have a library of cards organised in many files, like that of scribes and clerks, and whenever an angel finds itself in a new situation, it describes the situation to a Clerk Angel, who finds the appropriate card, and the card describes what the angel should do next. And the angel does it. And it happens with the speed of thought."

"Ha ha ha ha ... and do they have a name for this magic?"

"The angels employ the power of lightning harnessed to fine copper wire such as jewellers use in filigree. The lightning runs just as water does in irrigation channels, and there are sluices and gates and wheels — it is akin to the work of a mill-wright, but small, and with a mysterious fluid."

"And what is this fluid?"

"I know not. Some essence of lightning I am told, it is the blood of angels, their vital force, incomprehensible and mysterious. I am not a philosopher, just a Fool."

"You must talk to my brother. He has written a book imagining a world in which automata do all our menial tasks, freeing men and women for lives of untrammelled creativity."

The Prince of Staves was the most marvellous man the Fool had encountered. He was infused with energy and intelligence. Instantly she wanted his company, but feared he might find her ignorant and trivial. He was easy to meet. He supervised many public works around the City and would often take his ease in local taverns.

"And how is St. Ignatius?" asked the Fool.

"The roof timbers are decayed. Damp has found its way in and the worm has been at them. The mosaics in the chancel are some of the finest remaining from the First Empire and I am loath to see the Temple fall into decay and ruin."

"But can you not repair it?"

"I have some funds but too few carpenters and masons — there is a grave shortage of skilled labour. Craft masters have been much reduced by the plagues of recent years, and too many apprentices have been pressed to fight in our interminable wars. Now that the Coins and Cups have grown so wealthy they must all build palaces and be very grand, and they have the means to pay for the skills they require."

"Will not builders labour for love of the City? Is it not an honour to restore so fine a Temple?"

"The desire for wealth has become universal. When all are poor, men and women will labour out of love, but now that there are so many palaces, all have become greedy. Even guild journeymen aspire to dress in the courtly fashion and wear the best woollen hose and fasten fine feathers in their velvet caps. Their wives must have pearl nets in their hair. My funds will not stretch to luxuries. Alas, I must scour the City for craftsmen long retired with aches and pains and sore backs, and they direct young lads too poor to be apprentices. I fear many great buildings will become ruins."

"Would not better contrivances substitute for the labour of many?"

"Perhaps, if we had motive power. Wind and water mills are some-what inconvenient to transport through the city streets. Perhaps oxen, but war sets a high price on great numbers of oxen, and war procures the spoils to pay for them. All the oxen in the Empire would seem to be hauling the General and his baggage around the borderlands."

"I have heard tell of animate machines."

Prince of Staves

©C. A. L. 2017

223

"Ha ha ha. My sister says you have travelled to a place where they have such a thing?"

"I have — they look like angels."

"I expect they would. The ignorant see angels and mysteries where the wise see intelligible order and mechanism. So what did you learn about these automata?"

"They seem to perceive as we do. They see and hear. I cannot say whether they touch or taste or smell. They evaluate what they perceive using a great repository of rules, and then they act."

"How fascinating. They resemble clerics and legal scribes, who do nothing without first consulting a venerable tome. And where are the rules kept?"

"I do not know. This was not revealed."

"I saw an automaton recently, crafted with sublime skill to take the form of a young boy seated at a table, who drew pictures on a tablet. It was all mechanical of course, driven by cams."

"Prithee, what is a cam?" asked the Fool.

"A cam is an eccentric that rotates on a shaft and it is asymmetric so that as it rotates it moves something called a 'follower'. It converts the motion of a circle into a pushing and a pulling, like this."

"I have seen this in a mill! The shaft of the mill-wheel works a gate to release grain."

"Yes, that, but with an inconceivable complexity. You must imagine a complex system of cams and gears and shafts and levers configured to move the arm and hand of this mechanical boy, so that the hand draws a picture. To modify the picture one must configure an entirely different set of cams, a task that seems arduous in the extreme. But marvellous, extraordinary, no discounting the ingenuity of it.

"But — and here is the rub — no perception. This mechanical humanoid is entirely ignorant of one's presence. One might as well converse with a clockke, or a water wheel. And that is the nub is it not, being able to perceive, being able to discriminate between different situations, and so act differently?"

"My friend the Magician has said something similar."

"Yes, there is agreement among the wise: given motive power we can construct action of great complexity. But perception ... how do we achieve perception? Did your angels provide you with clues?"

"They did not, but I have been watching little beetles."

"Little beetles?"

"Wood-lice. I find them everywhere when I collect firewood. They congregate under dead wood."

"And rotten joists ... "

"They feel their way using feelers. They have a marvellous ability to find their way using feelers. Place dead wood on the ground in the evening and they will have found it come the light of morning."

"But they seem very limited?"

"They are clever at finding dead wood. What other goals they have I do not know."

"And your point is?"

"Well ... feelers. They find their way with feelers, much like a blind man with a stick. Suppose one had lots of little feelers that could move up and down, and then passed something underneath the feelers with holes cut in it. The feelers would move up and down as they moved across the holes."

"I see, like a music box, but reversed, with holes where the pins would be. So you cut holes in a piece of wood or a piece of card and move it underneath the feelers."

"Yes, yes, and you could have lots of cards, and chain the cards together, as long a chain as you want. And you can have many different card chains. You could even add new cards to the end of a chain."

"And what would these feelers do?"

"Go up and down and move things, like your cams."

"I see, and instead of having to devise new cams, one would only have to make holes in a card. Ingenious. But there is still no perception."

"There is if one can add new cards while it is working. Let us suppose one could cut cards to show whether a lock gate is open or closed, or a sluice raised or lowered, or the water in a pool low or high? The card becomes a mirror of the world, and my feelers can know what condition the gates and sluices and ponds are in. I could contrive a monstrous daemon of wood and iron to do the work of a miller."

"But this intermediacy of cards ... already windmills have devices to feather the sails in a gale, and I have seen mill ponds that worked their own sluices through floats and levers. There is no need for cards .... these cards seem complex and superfluous."

"But I see a principle: there is a part that discovers and shows what is true in the world, and a part that decides what to do, and they are separate, and communicate through a code, just as do a spy and a general."

"Yes, I see there is an abstract principle demonstrated, but I see also how far we are from seeing and hearing, from rational evaluation, and from speech, which are the signs of intelligence agreed by all philosophers of note. Discrimination, evaluation, good judgment, these are the fruits of perception, not some lever that works another lever."

The Fool felt deflated by this assessment. There was no malice in it. Her consistent experience of Staves was that they would listen to an idea, run it around in their heads, and if it fell short in any detail they would say so and often without tact. The most competent among them were so accustomed to this climate of brusque critique that rather than take umbrage, they would shrug amiably and cast about for a better idea. As one mason had explained to her, it was less humbling to watch an idea fall apart in a tavern than see a temple tower fall apart in ruin.

From time to time a youngster would come along with a grand new idea and the ancient grey-hairs of the craft would shake their heads and say it could not be done.

"Can't be done me young apprentice, ain't nuthin' as hasn't been tried back in the days of the good Empr'r Fortunus. Golden time that wus."

But it would be done, and the grey-hairs would study it carefully and pronounce that it was indeed quite obvious, and far from being an astonishing breakthrough, it must be one of the forgotten secrets from the golden age of the good Empr'r Fortunus.

The Fool and the Prince of Staves liked to meet in the Green Lion, a smaller tavern down a narrow lane off the Great Square. It was known for a powerful and fortifying dark ale much favoured by the market porters. One day the Prince of Staves and the Fool were sitting together drinking this powerful brew and the Fool said:

"The Staves are so ingenious and energetic and yet so poor. Why is that?"

The Prince looked dismayed.

"You raise an issue that concerns me deeply. The answer is simple to state. You will understand that the fundamental allegiance of the Coins is to wealth, possessions, and a life of luxury and ease. Likewise, the fundamental allegiance of the Swords is to ancestry, titles, honour, conquest and glory. The fundamental allegiance of the Cups is to that better part of the human spirit that cares for others, and the realisation of the Word of the Sun in this world."

The Fool nodded and the Prince continued. "The fundamental allegiance of the Staves is to the labour of our hands and minds, and the tangible betterment of this world. We delight that we can grow and build and make. Like vain little gods, we look at what we have made and see that it is good. For us, purpose and pleasure derives from making. We are satisfied to grow our own food, build our own houses, build boats and catch our own fish, weave our clothes, fire our own pots, raise sheep, goats, and cattle, drink our own wine, and sleep in beds crafted from wood we have cut. This is our delight. For those of us with the temperament, this is a good way to live."

"And so it is. I much admire this independence and pleasure in simple things."

"But there is a problem. Perhaps there was once a golden age with sufficient land for all. This is what we read in Damasio's *Chronicle of the First Empire*. Each family could eat their fill, and there were forests filled with game, and an abundance of timber for building and burning. This is no longer so. The land has been divided and sub-divided until a plot can barely support a family. Our noble Swords have seized large tracts of forest as private domains for their interminable hunts, and they have claimed ownership of much land that was once owned in common, so that the inhabitants have become tenants and serfs; or worse still, they are forced off the land and become the poorest dwellers in our sprawling cities. Taxes and tithes are set so high that people are forced to borrow from Coins during poor seasons, and if they default in the face of ruinous interest, their land is forfeit. Once land is seized, it can be amalgamated into great estates and farmed efficiently so that even fewer are required on the land, and those who remain are little better than slaves. Staves are being continuously oppressed, displaced, and forced off their land through poverty and starvation."

"I encounter this everywhere. It is iniquitous."

"And still we labour with our hearts and minds. We make swords and armour for the Swords so that they can oppress us further. We build grand houses for the Coins. We build churches and temples for the Cups, weave and embroider their vestments, and craft their gold and silver, so that they can tell us that our meekness, poverty and suffering will be rewarded — but not in this world. As a class we are absurdly foolish, the instruments of our own oppression. If they think of us at all, it is that we are a rabble, stupid and uneducated.

"And there is an issue that occupies my mind. It is that we will never cease from looking for ways to make our situation worse than it is. If there is a way to carry out a task more efficiently, then we will find it. I see this every day. The potter, the miller, the weaver, the baker, the seamstress, the wheelwright, the carriage builder, the mariner, the printer, the smith: every craft is a ferment of invention and innovation. Each day I hear of new techniques, speedier assembly, finer work. There is a workshop of a weapon-smith where each journeyman makes but one component, for months. Each part must fit unseen with every other part, every crossbow identical. All this so that the master may become wealthy, selling ten bows where every other master sells one. He grows wealthy from the labour of those he is charged to teach and train. This master may soon resemble the Coins in doing nothing more each day than admiring his fine house. His children will marry well, and live idly, looking down on poor Staves who went blind making brass wheel-locks."

"So what will happen?"

"Revolution! Can you not feel it? The energy, the discontent? Why should we labour for the Swords and Coins and Cups and yet be poor and despised? We are many, and we are skilled and accustomed to labour and long days. We can make a new army, and terrible new weapons. We can build terrible new ships. We will take the great estates and give them to the poor. The Coins will discover how genuinely useless they are, and the Swords will discover that the castles we built for them can be ruined even more quickly with the powder my sister has brought from the East. And the Cups will learn that we are capable of being happy in this world without the need of some future paradise!"

The Fool was dismayed. She had seen the handbills and heard the speeches. She had witnessed a succession of turbulent young men being dragged to the great tree on the hill outside the City, and hung for sedition. She did feel the energy and she did feel the discontent. The Prince looked downcast.

"And so we will rule the Empire. There will be a world of abundance. And yet I fear will we will still be our own worst enemies. We will make better tools and better processes ... and what is the best tool and the best process?"

"A legion of angels?" suggested the Fool. "We can watch the angels sweep our floors and bake our bread and they will never grow weary or quarrelsome because they are eternal and without souls."

"Indeed. We can make perfect machines for every task. We will have an automaton that picks fruit, and harvests corn, and weaves cloth, and cuts stone, and then what is there for us to do. We will all be as idle and worthless as Coins."

"Do not say that. I am idle and a Fool, but surely not worthless?"

"Alas, a melancholy is in me, and my words are out of sort. This dark brew infects my wits and makes me dull and distempered."

The Queen of Staves had a controversial reputation arising from her opinions on design. She funded and supervised extraordinary new work in ceramics, glassware and furniture in a workshop complex located in a converted watermill close to the City. Her thesis was that beauty was not created by a superfluity of extraneous decoration "randomly applied as if by a child playing with mud". This remark was directed at the Princess of Coins, the principal exponent of a new style in which extraneous decoration was invariably applied to excess. According to the Queen, beauty was to be found in the materials themselves, and it was the task of the artist and artisan to reveal that beauty in simple and functional forms.

"One should not," she said, "conceal it under a riot of extraneous detail crafted purely to demonstrate that one has read a book with romantic or fanciful themes". This remark was aimed not only at the Princess of Coins but at the burgeoning, bourgois *nouveau-riche* in society, who sought to demonstrate a familiarity with the classics by covering every surface from the floor boards to the rooftops with gilt-and-plaster scenes from antiquity.

"The Coins need to show that they are special, a breed apart from the common folk, and so everything they possess must be elaborated beyond the reach of the common folk that they are. They do not have a pedigree, and so they must have gilt and filigree. They must stick

QUEEN OF STAVES

©·A·L·2017

another ten ribbons and bows on a dress, and keep the poor, half-blind lace-makers busy in their hovels — so poor they can scarce afford the tallow to work through the night. The Coins do so enjoy seeing poor people work hard. Heaven forbid that there could be beauty in something simple."

"I am simple," said the Fool.

"I suspect this is the great jest you play upon the world," said the Queen. "Tell me, do you find the world beautiful or ugly?"

"Beautiful," said the Fool.

"Interesting. I find the question to be a test of temperament. Many people find the world a place of beauty and care for it, but some find it ugly and unbearable and care nothing about despoiling it and using it to their own advantage."

"I find the souls of some people ugly," said the Fool.

"On that we can agree. The world that people make for themselves is a reflection of their souls. If there is ugliness and confusion and vanity in the soul, then whether it be architecture, painting, poesy, song or apparel, we will find ugliness there too. Is that not why the Muses adhere so closely to the Sun? There is a Sun within us, and that is where we find beauty, elegance, proportion, and harmony. Before creating anything in this world we should first inspect our own souls, for that determines the character of our work. Come, let us walk."

They walked, and the Queen showed the Fool works of great simplicity and beauty.

"As I am a Fool, it is in my nature to be foolish your Majesty, and so I hope you will forgive me when I say that I love embellishment ... when it comes from the power of imagination, for I dearly love stories."

"You speak of the narrative impulse in art, the impulse to give life to the imagination through decoration?"

"Yes," your Majesty.

"And so every plate, ewer, vase, book, and wall should be so covered in decoration that all we see is ourselves reflected back at us, a distortion of our face in every surface? As if stories were the entire substance of the world?"

"I did not wish to give offence your Majesty."

"It is a common offence, and one I struggle with daily. I do not abhor the notion — the Cups make great use of stained glass in the Temples to instruct the poor who cannot read, and these are works of singular beauty. The intention there is clear however, and different in effect from a chamber-pot covered in nymphs."

"So one could have a book of pictures if the entire book was the embodiment of a *worthwhile* tale?"

"I struggle against images Mistress Fool. Imagination has a freedom that the world does not possess, and when embodied, imagination is made gross and lumpen, and Substance, an unwilling receptacle, is sullied and obscured. It seems to me that imagination rests well upon the talents of the storyteller and poet, like a bird that lights gently on a branch. As for Substance, poor child of Necessity, I seek to elevate Substance so that it declares, nay shouts, its inner beauty."

"But a book of pictures ..."

"This thing intrigues you."

"Yes your Majesty. Each sense has a power to enchant. The Cups understand this well: song, sermon, sweet perfume of incense, bells, storytelling in glass and light;. Imagination rests lightly not just on the singular power of words but on each sense, separately and together. And so ... a book of pictures ... to enchant the eyes."

"You have given this thought?"

"It is the natural gift of the Fool to observe the contribution of each sense upon the mood of a company, lest we neglect our audience and entertain only for ourselves. Is it not said that 'Folly is a practice as full of labour as a wise man's art'?"

"And so, a book of images ... it would harness the imagination through image alone, or employ image as an accessory to a written text?"

"Perhaps through image alone, but with artifice, so that words spring freely to the mind, and the story constructs itself afresh each time the book is read?"

"Interesting. And would there be beauty in this book of pictures?"

"As you say, your Majesty, beauty is an aspect of the soul, and art its reflection."

"Tell me Mistress Fool, what is the beauty of the soul. How does one discern it?"

"Forgive me your Majesty, I am a mere Fool."

"But if pressed to answer?"

"Then it is when the soul is straight and of one purpose, and not crooked and contending with itself. When the soul has the restraint of Virtue and is not driven by lust and desire to act only for its own benefit. When a soul has a clear view of itself and its motives and is not misdirected by vanity and self-deception."

"And how came you to this understanding?"

"In the mountains, a Hermit, a man of philosophical reflection ..."

"Ah, the old Emperor Aloysius. It seems he has found some wisdom in solitude."

"You know of him your Majesty?"

"I curtsied to him in the Imperial Court when he was still Emperor. I was but a child, and that was a long time ago. The Emperor I knew was not a kindly man. He vanished, many thought he was dead. He was not missed. Now he is merely a name in the chronicles of Empire."

"He died but recently."

"You knew him well?"

"I did your Majesty."

"Then my condolences. And what of his philosophy? It survives?"

"He wrote a book on the quest for Virtue. I have it here."

"This is his hand?"

"It is."

"Most elegant. The calligraphy of a cultured man. And this

'Miranda' in the dedication?"

"I cannot say."

"I recall he had a daughter. Or perhaps not. It must be forty years since the end of his reign, and we have had two Emperors since. Perhaps grandchildren. We have all grown old, alas. What is the thesis of this work?"

"It is a study of virtue and vice, and how the unmitigated quality of vanity, ambition and greed brings harm to others. And how we should be steadfast in ourselves and show kindness in spite of the trials and tribulations of Fortune, not being jubilant at the rising of the Wheel, arrogant at the peak, or despondent at the fall."

"A philosophical work by an Emperor — now there is a thing of immutable novelty. And this work, is it worthy of publication?"

"I believe so."

"If you leave it with me, I will consult with a printer."

"Thank you your Majesty."

Once again the Fool was supping ale with the Prince of Staves, and much enjoying the company. The Prince was still supervising the renovation of the roof of St. Ignatius.

"Tomorrow I leave to visit Father," said the Prince. "Would you like to accompany me? Do you ride? I can arrange a horse. It is but half a day, and a pleasing ride along the Ripian Way."

"I would be most honoured. As for riding, I have been confined to the back of a mule for many arduous leagues and although I have no finesse, I would enjoy a gentle pace. Will your Father enjoy the company of a Fool?"

"My father is the most noble and generous of men and would sit down in a pigsty and charm the pigs if he thought they were lonely or upset."

"And would he would extended this magnanimity even to a Fool?"

"Sometimes my speech comes out other than I intend."

KING OF STAVES

©C. A. L. 2017

The Ripian Way was an ancient paved road flanked by decaying memorials and tombs of the most extravagant kind. It possessed the quality of a dream that seems more real than life. The Prince had found a gentle and tractable horse for the Fool and they cantered through a landscape of ancient stone and impossible romance.

"Tell me more of your Father," said the Fool.

"His great passion is the improvement of land and the welfare of his tenants. And animals. Few things disturb him more than the ill-treatment of animals. His tenants have learned to be scrupulous in their welfare. He has little care for wealth, but such is the happy commerce of his estates, there is a general prosperity among all. He spends most of his days roaming around on an old cart."

"An old cart?"

"It amuses him. Some kings grant audiences from a high throne in a great room. My father prefers the countryside. Anyone walking the roads can share the bench seat of his cart and discuss anything, from the lateness of spring to the plague of moles disturbing the pasture. You may have met him unawares."

"It is likely that I have."

Your Majesty!" said the Fool.

"Ha, my favourite Fool! I was not a Majesty before, so we will have none of that now. Call me Father and I will call you Daughter and we will cause consternation as far as the Great Sea. Have you found yourself some better boots? You were in some discomfort when last we met upon the road."

"I know a shoemaker in the city ... Father, a man of some education, who exchanges boots for the instruction of his children in the simpler matters of music and song."

"Then you are well shod. Excellent. Come, let me show you the garden. It is my great pleasure."

They roamed around the garden which, unusually for a regal estate, was as rich in fruit and vegetables as it was in flowers and ornamental paths. They paused at a small meadow divided into several plots.

"This is my great secret!" said the King. "You know that a good farmer lets a field lie fallow for a year? That soil is drained of vitality, like a well that is over-drawn, and must have time to restore its quality?"

"I know little of these things."

"I measure the yield of this little field and plant it with many fallow crops to see which is best in restoring the soil. Then I count the yield from each plot. It seems that peas and beans and clover are most beneficial. And one can eat the peas!"

"This is the work of a lifetime."

"And most well spent, most well spent! Through the arts of husbandry my farms are more prosperous, and my tenants can invest in water channels for when the rains fail. We have more mills, there is a spirit of progress and invention. Our smiths and carpenters are well employed with skilled work. All it takes is an interest in the craft of farming. Every silver piece that is gained from the land is spent in the villages and towns, and all trades prosper. What better use of a life than to benefit a thousand lives with simple discoveries requiring only occasional diligence ... and still I have much leisure."

"You are a Father to your people. You instruct them in what is best."

"I will not deny it. It gives me satisfaction. Tell me the news."

"There is much war along the border."

"As always. War is good for soldiers — at least, for those who triumph and plunder, and return home with limbs intact. Not so for farmers. Have you travelled in Illyria?"

"Their harvest was burned and there is no cheer and little food. Charity has disappeared and I cannot sustain myself."

"These wars cause scarcity and drive up the price of food everywhere. The abbeys and manors have no shortage, but the common folk are suffering. I must see the Emperor."

"He will see you?"

"He will, but he listens to many voices. War is an excellent business for some, and there is much profit in it. What other news?"

"These is a great turmoil among the common folk. It has become the fashion to read and purchase fine books. They have all become theologians. You will know this I am sure; assemble three market-day scholars in one place and you will have three new opinions on ancient doctrines, and a priest shouting heresy and calling for the stake. There has been a great bonfire of books in the City. It is universally agreed that this turmoil is the fault of Fra. Maximo Biasi, who translated the Sacred Books into the Common Tongue and gave them to the printers to play with. I hear he has taken refuge in the farthest east of Illyria."

"I think even Illyria will be too small to contain the outrage of the Church. He must seek some further refuge where goose feathers have never seen ink, and books are used for the cooking fire and the latrine. You are uncommonly good company for a Fool. Tomorrow is the day of the monthly Petty Court where I hear disputes and make judgements. Will you sit with me? I ask only that for one day you set aside your Fool's cap, for my tenants will not be judged by a Fool."

"I will Father."

The Fool set aside her cap, borrowed some clothes, and once again assumed a remarkable resemblance to the Princess Bianca. From the South.

"What shall we call you?" asked the King.

"Princess Bianca Father. My birth father was deprived of his land in the south by a villainous brother."

"Splendid! One could almost imagine you were born to this sort of thing. I think you will enjoy this tribunal — all the drama of the farm condensed into a morning of grievous complaint."

The first case was that of cows wandering into an adjacent field, eating the crop, and dying of bloat. One farmer wanted compensation for the damaged crop. The other wanted compensation for the dead cows. Both insisted the damaged fence was not their responsibility. The King turned and looked at the Princess Bianca.

"The first purpose of the fence in this case is to retain the cows. The cows have died in great pain. It does not matter whose fence it is, the farmer with the cows has failed in his care."

"I agree. That will be the judgement."

The farmer with the cows was ordered to pay compensation for the crops, with an additional fine that went to the support of the poor.

The next case was that of a well-known drunkard who had spent his money on ale, and had gone out in the dead of night to steal vegetables to feed his family.

"Difficult," said the King quietly.

"We should not punish a wife and children."

"And yet he blackmails us with their need. This is not the first time." The King turned to the room. "One month hard labour in the quarry. If there is any drinking, two months. The court will care for the family."

The morning continued. A group of village elders crowded the court claiming (quite improbably) that their boundary stones had been moved. A tavern owner was accused of short measures. A dog had been sold and run back to its owner. A horse had died the day after the sale. A barn had caught fire, and neighbours accused.

Well, Daughter, we must do this more often," said the King. "If ever you tire of wearing out good boots, come and keep an old man in company with his tribunals and his judgements."

"Yes Father," said the Fool.

# ❧23❧

# THE PRINCE OF CUPS

*In which Charity begins at home.*

The Fool and the Empress were sitting together in the garden playing with Baba the little fox, who was no longer so little but still extremely playful.

"She pounces like a cat," laughed the Fool. "Her appearance is that of a dog, but her play is that of a cat. She is most endearing."

"I love her so," said the Empress, "and fear for her every day. The common folk of this estate were raised to detest foxes. The dogs are trained to kill. I fear that she will wander. You must see many foxes as you travel?"

"I do, but they are shy, for as you say, they are much persecuted and fear humankind. When I rise at dawn the far country is full of life — badgers, rabbits, hares, hedgehogs, deer, boar, bears, wolves, and foxes. Sometimes I see otters and voles at play by the rivers, and beavers working along the banks. There are cats, timid and fierce, but rarely seen."

"I would so love to see these creatures. With all my heart I would love to see them in their own worlds."

"Is there not a zoo your Highness?"

"It pains me to see them so confined and ill-used for entertainment."

"The common folk see either a meal or an opportunity for sport. One must travel far to see the wilder things in abundance and without fear."

"I would that you could take me! Far into the wild, and we could sit and sing to them, and they would come to us and be without fear. Would you?"

"I fear that an Imperial procession with all its pomp and noise might be inimical to the goal you seek your Highness."

"We must steal away by night on fast horses and be far gone into the wild."

"The entire realm has a duty to preserve you from harm, your Highness. Should you sneak away, I fear the hullabaloo of horns and knights and dogs, and the random blunderings of watches and militias, would startle every wild thing within an hundred leagues and disturb even the long dead."

"You are much too practical for a Fool, but I fear you are right. I would not want the long dead to stumble blindly among the living on my account. Perhaps I could have a lodge in the wild, and a few kindly folk to tend it and some men-at-arms to guard it and ward off hunters and brigands. We could go there and rise at dawn, and not be a cause of alarm to an entire Empire. I will talk to my husband. Yes, you may smile, but in every small thing I have to temper romance with the reality of my life."

"I pray that you may have this little thing your Highness."

"I do envy your freedom. I am permitted anything except what I most desire."

"The romance of my life is also tempered with much reality your

Majesty. My freedom is mixed with cold nights, stormy weather, and hard ground. The common folk are kind, but there are many days when I know I am stealing food from their plates. There are many more days when there is no food to be had and I forage for remnants of nuts and acorns that the squirrels have missed. I boil nettles and stuff my mouth full of dandelions. I wade in ponds and pull up waterlily roots with my toes. I fish. I could trap and snare but I do not , for there are too many petty lords who love to hang poachers, and besides, I have grown too fond of the little creatures of this world."

"We must feed you then. Do you not fear brigands?"

"They know I have less than they do. Often they feed me in return for news and a jolly evening."

"They do not desire to ... take you?"

"I suppose they might, but men are a curious mix of impulses. They will force themselves on one woman, and yet die to protect the honour of another."

"They protect you as might a brother?"

"Curious is it not? I am safer on the road than in town or castle. Besides, I have some talent with a knife. I have entertained many, and have chastened (as does the spiky porcupine) those who sought to devise their own entertainments."

"You must show me these talents, not having witnessed this marvellous porcupine."

"Your guard has deprived me of my playthings your Highness."

"Some other day then."

"Willingly your Highness. And how is your son?"

"Being nursed by a regiment of nannies and maids. I cannot do anything right. I am tut-tutted and shooshed and patronised until I desire to order executions. But he is well, and he is growing teeth and growing unruly, and the Emperor is pleased."

A servant came and whispered to the Empress. The Empress turned to the Fool.

"I have a meeting with the Prince of Cups. I would like to introduce you."

"Of course your Highness."

The Prince of Cups was a man in his late twenties, and dressed in a plain black cassock of superior cut and fabric.

"Your Majesty, my most profuse thanks for granting me the gift of your time, and if I may say, you look more beautiful than ever. I am astonished. In this *most exquisite* of gardens there is not a flower so fair!" He bowed with a great flourish.

"You flatter, your Excellency."

"No no, no, most decidedly I do not! I am impelled to lavish praise your Majesty, for I cannot contain my feeling. I must not stand accused of mere flattery."

"Then you are forgiven," the Empress laughed. "Your Eminence, I would like you to meet my good friend and companion, who travels the roads and ways of the Empire in the guise of a Fool."

"I am most honoured your Eminence, and there is no guise. I am entirely Foolish, and none who know me well would dispute this."

"And most fair of face and form too I see. I am most fortunate to make your acquaintance."

"Why, thank you your Eminence," said the Fool, who had taken an instant dislike to the man.

A train of servants arrived bearing furniture and drinks and sweetmeats and pastries until there were refreshments for a village. There followed an extended courtly ritual of light conversation and pleasantries, in which the Prince was effusive with flattery and charm.

"He is most gallant is he not?" said the Empress to the Fool.

"Most gallant your Highness."

"You seem low in spirit?" the Empress observed.

"I am overwhelmed with food, and my mouth is stopped. Like the serpent, I enter torpor and will sleep for a month."

"Never a serpent," said the Prince. "You are too fair to bear

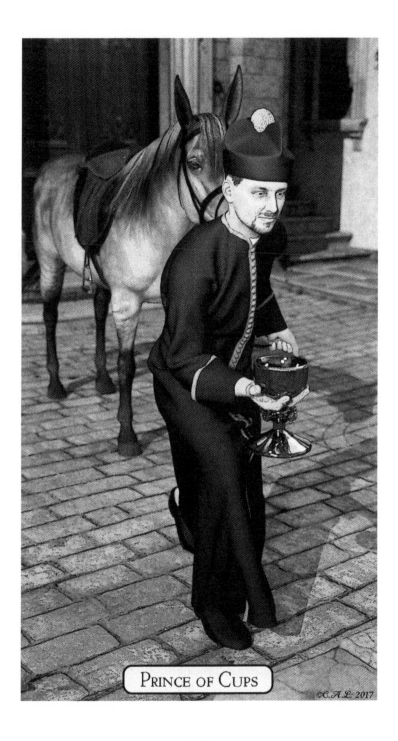

PRINCE OF CUPS

©C.A.L. 2017

comparison with a foul and sly creature that slithers in the dirt."

"Perhaps I am both fair and foul, with a mask of fairness and the heart of a serpent?" said the Fool.

"You jest of course," smiled the Prince.

"She is kind and has the voice of an angel," said the Empress.

"Your Eminence," said the Fool, "is it not said that of all the creatures only the serpent could feel the anguish of the Devil, and the serpent was one creature in Heaven and Earth with true sympathy?"

"Sympathy for the Devil, only the Devil, a partnership of evil that accomplished the ruin of perfection," said the Prince.

"Then should we despise the Devil for his anguish? Is there perfection when one being is in pain?"

"Perhaps your travel has brought you acquaintance with a false doctrine?" said the Prince with a frown.

"Forgive me your Eminence, I am as much a Fool as my cap declares."

"Your visit," said the Empress to the Prince, discharging the tension, "It is doubtless in connection with your works for the benefit of the poor and dispossessed?"

"An orphanage," your Majesty. "A home for the street children of the City, for there are many that sleep in doorways and ruins and sell themselves for food and clothing. They have no instruction in good conduct or the doctrines of the Church, and when grown, are a burden to the constables and the courts. If you should permit it, this orphanage will bear your name and stand as a sign of the dignity and culture of your reign."

"What say you?" the Empress asked the Fool. "You must be familiar with the travails of these poor orphans?"

"Indeed your Highness. What they desire most is to be loved and cared for, to have a place that is safe, and people who are kind and love them. Instruction and decency come naturally to the young when their welfare is assured, and they witness kindness in daily life."

"There you have it your Eminence, a Fool that speaks the thoughts of an Empress. Will they be loved?"

"Love is the first doctrine of the Temple your Highness."

"And how is this great work to be achieved?"

"Through the greatest of all virtues, Charity. I thought perhaps a great ball, held in your name. The greatest in the land would attend if you were to host such a ball, and the success of this cause would be assured."

"A great ball? For charity, for the aid of those who suffer? How novel!" said the Empress.

"I thought perhaps a masque your Majesty. A great Folly ... in these distressing times, a diversion, and for the most worthy of purposes."

"A Folly ... yes, this court is burdened with a great seriousness of purpose, and some diversion might be a worthy distraction. But I wonder whether our stolid councillors and stern soldiers and dour court officials would be at ease with frivolity? The Emperor himself is tireless in devotion to the Empire and I beg him to relax and be at ease, but he works while the owls hoot and the dogs howl and often until the cock crows. He will grudge the time and I fear he might lower the mood and sully any attempt at the frivolous. I must consult with my husband. But a ball ... yes, let us have a ball. It is the duty of an Emperor to be generous and entertain, and we can promote your good causes and shame the court into generosity." She turned to the Fool. "As Mistress of Folly, perhaps you can advise?"

"We must accept and give thanks that we are governed by those of sober disposition. They may struggle to make merry, but they are diligent in administration. It is said that just as your court governs the Empire, so the power of the starry firmament governs the soul your Highness. Those ruled by Venus are quick to make merry, and those ruled by Saturn tend to discipline and work but also melancholy and solitude. It is the rule of the Heavens, and with that we cannot contend.

"But perhaps I can suggest entertainments to distract and lighten sober minds? There is a travelling troupe whose comedies would unravel dour Saturn himself and have even the old one roaring with mirth. And a masque may be welcome to those who have worn a sober face for too long and may wish to wear another."

The Prince nodded vigorously. "These are points well made your Majesty."

"Indeed. I will consult with my husband and you may arrange to meet with me again."

"It seems you have a wise Fool your Majesty. And she sings like an angel?"

"We sing together, your Eminence," said the Fool. Women have many accomplishments beyond face and form."

"Indeed you do, indeed you do ..."

"Shall we sing your Highness, 'The White Ship', in two parts of harmony."

The Empress looked amused but also diffident, and seemed about to refuse, then saw the resolve on her friend's face.

"Yes, let us sing ... 'The White Ship'."

They sang 'The White Ship' together. It told of a ship that carried the heroic dead across the sea to a Blessed Isle beyond the sunset. They sang with obvious pleasure and communion of spirit, and servants and gardeners ceased labour, for although they had become familiar with the voices, the Fool and the Empress were accomplished. His Eminence wilted visibly at the focus of their attention, for it was not his custom to lose control of a gathering. After he had been effusive in praise and made his departure the Empress burst out laughing.

"He was only being gallant. It is a courtly affectation."

"He dismissed me. I could see it in his eyes. And not even because I am a Fool! Because I am a woman."

"He did. He conceals his nature with a great show and display, and he deserved his punishment. Come, have you eaten enough? I am sure we can find more."

"Thank you your Highness, but if I could fill my bag for the road."
More food was brought, and the Fool took it all, for she knew she
would share it along the way.

"Where do you go?"

"The Sheep Fair in the City. And I have friends to see."

"Fare ye well Fool, and return soon."

"May you be blessed and safe your Highness."

Nine days later The Fool was supping ale in a City tavern with the
Prince of Staves.

"Have you heard the news," said the Prince. "The General, against
whom you fulminate whenever you are in your cups, has been stricken
down. Physicians say his heart failed — fell stone dead off his horse into
a slough of mud. The campaign is stalled. There is talk of a treaty."

"I know not whether to thank Fortune or Justice."

"Or the pharmacopoeia of the wise. There are rumours."

"This merits more ale," said the Fool, "Much more. Barkeep! And
speaking of Cups, I met the Prince of that ilk."

"Then Fortune deals us the same hand, for so did I," replied the
Prince.

"You met the Prince?"

"He is building an extraordinary palace in the hills and desires
the greatest water garden in the world. He asked me to advise on the
construction of a system of aqueducts, pools, tunnels, leats, pipes and
valves to supply the fountains."

"He is building a palace?"

"He has entirely drained the Empire of painters and gilders. I hear
the Princess of Coins is wandering through unfinished halls empty of
labour."

"I feel for her. She has a kind heart even though it is unbalanced by
a furor of extravagance."

"This new palace will be incomparable, a great wonder of the age. And how did a mere Fool come to meet with so great a Prince?"

"He walks among us extolling Charity as the greatest of virtues. He is raising a fund for an orphanage in the city."

"Ah yes, hospitals, almshouses for the aged, orphanages, and the restoration of churches. The man is tireless in his passion for good causes. He moves among us like a saint, inspiring us to give freely that the divine benevolence of the Sun shine equally on all."

"It seems the Sun shines on him more equally than many."

"Charity begins at home."

"What an odious man," exclaimed the Fool.

"Entirely," laughed the Prince.

# ✎24✎

# THE STAR

*In which we find the Star is Down to Earth.*

ood morning Urania!"

"Good morning Miranda. I see that you wear the jingling cap, and yet it is said that you have ceased to be a Fool?"

"And who is the source of these rumours?"

"I cannot recall. Perhaps it was Clio."

"In that case I am a Fool Emeritus."

"You jest! There is such a thing?"

"Just as there are fools who play at being wise, so there are wise heads who play at being fools."

"And what is it that you play?"

"I play the whistle. See? And I hop and skip and have such scarce dignity that I must indeed be a Fool."

"That is a merry tune you play, but you caper with the grace of a spider on a griddle. I judge you still a Fool. And how may I help?"

"I journeyed with the Moon for a night ... and saw much ... and understood little. I thought to meet the Star."

"And if I may enquire why?"

"I seek to understand Necessity, and the Moon is so far removed from Necessity that my mind is all in confusion. I thought the Star, being steady like the Sun and accustomed to the flighty and wayward natures of stars, might restore my wits for me."

"Ah, stars! How they love to tax my patience. GEMINI!" she screamed, "Cease your endless chatter, you rise in five! To the East! NOW! I have been instructing Canis Major to herd them together like so many sheep."

"And do they? Assemble?"

"Yes. For all the noise and confusion, they do rise. I feel this indiscipline is merely an amusement at my expense."

"And I may see the Star?"

"Yes, you should see her. The Star is set, and you will find her in her mansion ... o'er there."

"That one? By the stream?"

"Yes."

"And I may go? Is there ought I should know?"

"She is kindly and well disposed."

The Star's mansion had the style of an ancient country villa of four sides around a central courtyard. In the courtyard there was a large pool with reeds and moss and stones and water lilies, fed by a leat from the nearby stream. The Star had the soft and fragile beauty of a moth or butterfly. She was seated on a rock, singing a quiet song, and much absorbed in pouring a strange essence into the pool from two silver ewers.

"Ah, my favourite Fool. Sit with me."

"You know me?"

"There is a star who watches over you."

"There is? I would know of it."

"Then you must call your angel, and you will be directed."

XVII THE STAR

©C.A.L. 2017

"I have an angel too?"

"Oh yes ... have you not met your angel? Consult with your friend the Magician, he has the formula — I gave it to him myself. And how may I help you?"

"I journeyed with the Moon, seeking to understand Necessity, but all I discovered is that one comprehends little while under the Moon's tutelage."

"Yes, a wild ride indeed. And so you come to me?"

"Please, if you can spare the time, most glorious luminosity!"

"If you seek my advice, then here it is. You should relinquish your infatuation with Necessity."

"But ..."

"I can feel the urgency in you. You could be idling and Fooling and finding beauty, and yet here you are filled with urgency, knocking on my door, requiring audience, seeking clarification. There is a power of Necessity in you."

"I seek to understand the weight of evil in the world."

"And soon you will be hastening to rectify it. You will rush hither and thither on endless tasks, resisting counsel or restraint, filled with an irresistible urgency. You will come to despise innocent Foolery. You will lecture with a stern visage: 'We must do this' and 'We must do that', as if a grave responsibility for the future of the entire Cosmos had become yours."

"And so I should be idle? I am to be without purpose? I must leave evil to its own devices? What of those who are oppressed and must toil from dusk till dawn? Who have families to feed, and cannot rest for even one Sun's width of time? How are they to evade Necessity?"

"And is it you who oppress them?"

"No ..."

"And is it a necessity that they should be so oppressed?"

"No ..."

"And are they oppressed because of human greed?"

"For the most part, yes."

"And naturally you desire that this should not be so. You rail at Necessity, for now you understand how terrible and broken and ugly the world is. You have supped with the Devil, and caught his anger and despite. You are done with Fooling. In place of innocence and joy you are afflicted with an urgency, and this urgency drives you forward like an ox that is goaded."

"It is true that I feel a sense of alarm and urgency. What soil gives rise to these feelings?" asked the Fool.

"Sympathy. Injustice. A kind heart. You are oppressed by the sight of evil. In your vanity you think to remedy what the Sun and the Moon and the stars could not. Understand this: Necessity never wanted evil. Necessity desires beauty, a perfectly crafted and harmonious Cosmos. But the Devil demanded freedom, and so we have evil. But it is not Necessity that makes evil, and not the Devil either. It is the human soul, aping Necessity. The impulse to organise, to control, to subdue, driven by greed and ambition and vanity."

"You see that impulse in me? That I would be Emperor of some small empire?"

"Know thyself."

"Then should I be as the Hermit? Retiring in solitude to rectify the ambition in my soul?"

"I like you better as a Fool. How else can joy flow into the world? It must be sought out, like a rare treasure. Come, walk with me, I would show you the garment of Necessity, the robe that She wears." They walked around the pool. "Look, here ... in the water ... can you see?"

"In faith, so beautiful ... like stars and flowers and sea creatures," said the Fool, marvelling.

"These are the symmetries. Necessity desired simplicity and elegance and beauty. Symmetry is simple because once you have seen a part you can make the whole ... like folding a parchment and cutting it with shears to make pretty shapes, as children sometimes do. Cut a quarter and you have the whole pattern. These patterns are best seen through the inner eye of the higher mind, through geometry and algebra. Then the beauty is unfolded, like a precious garment that has been hidden in a cupboard and brought forth into the light. Symmetry is Chaos subdued and ordered. You are acquainted with these arts?"

"The Magician has shown me his books, but I lack his insight. I did not think you would be so learned and philosophical."

"Philosophers supplicate for my instruction, but I withhold my attention, for few are worthy. To the chosen I teach geometry and symmetry. To the less worthy I teach optics and the science of measurement, and they make instruments of brass and crystal to delineate me more clearly. They enumerate and catalogue my stars. They spy on my transits, and I reward them with morsels and scraps from my table."

"What is this pool?"

"It is the Mirror of the World."

"And what do you pour into it?"

"Life."

"Life? And what is this Life?"

"Life is Folly, the germ that upsets Necessity. The young are entirely Folly, and that is why they run to greet you in every town and village. The young love Folly. They are raised up from Folly and schooled in the ways of Necessity, so that they may be adults, and wrapped in so many layers of stricture that the Folly of old age is like a corpse in its grave windings. Death comes to them and unwraps the soul for me. I listen to the soul (for now it recalls itself) and if it so wishes I return it to the world so it can be young again, and foolish."

The Fool was silent for a time. "This is not the common opinion of Folly. Scholars disparage Folly. Scholars speak of Folly as a spirit of ignorance, of a failure to comprehend cause and effect, a preening vanity and high opinion of oneself that causes harm (and yet sees none of it), like a dog that wags its tail and breaks the best jug."

"You are wounded by this opinion?" asked the Star.

XXI NECESSITY

©C.A.L 2017

"Yes."

"But you are not that kind of Fool. I would not see you if you were that kind of Fool."

"There is more to Folly?"

"You know that there is. There is the Folly of ignorance and vanity and narrow self-absorption that is scorned by philosophers. There is also a living spirit of action and invention, play and joyful communion, that defies Necessity. It has the appearance of Folly to those who have a place in the world and do not wish their comfort to be disturbed. In their eyes only a Fool would defy Necessity. Perhaps your scholars have spent too long with their books? They see Folly everywhere but not in their self-absorption?"

They sat together and looked into the pool. Necessity was indeed beautiful.

"I was mistaken. The garment of Necessity is sublime. May I pour some souls into the world?"

"You may."

The Fool took one of the silver ewers and poured it onto the waters. Souls swam out, like so many tiny fish.

"They look frightened."

"They have forgotten themselves and they are helpless."

"Why do they forget?"

"They must inhabit a form from the realm of Necessity, and so they forget their place in the sky."

"As I have forgotten?"

"As you have forgotten."

"I wanted to ask you a question."

"Please ask."

"When I ran with the Moon, and when I danced with the Moon, the Moon was still in the sky."

"Celestials are not bound by Necessity. For us there is no time and no space."

"And yet you converse, you have a human form, and you act and move as if you had substance."

"I can converse with a thousand Fools at the same instant, argue a thousand points, shine from a myriad of stars. I am not bound to a place in space or bound to a place in time."

"There are other Stars?"

"There are no other Stars. We are One. Perhaps you have seen a ray of sunshine strike a crystal lustre, and a dozen rainbows move around the room. Necessity is the lustre that fractures my unity, and yet I am ever One."

"And yet you are here with me now, not present as a stone is present, inert and timeless, but present as a living being. We converse ..."

"And you struggle with the particularity of my conversation, the insistence that I am *here!* and *now!*"

"Yes."

"I am fractured by Necessity but not bound as you are. When you are divided in opinion or purpose, you are in conflict within yourself. You love someone ... and yet you hate them. You enjoy luxury, but you despise wealth. You enjoy ale, and dislike the person you become. You want to stay where you are. You desire to go somewhere else. These warring inclinations within your being are forced to inhabit the same house, like a family that wars with itself.

"Celestial beings are not inwardly divided and confined in antagonism as you are. Each warring inclination causes separation, one being becomes two, becomes four, becomes eight, eight becomes a multitude, until there is no more division, and each atom of being has but one undivided purpose. Being indivisible it cannot be deflected or changed. It is eternally what it is, and that is Substance, the garment of Necessity. Necessity is the end of Being."

"But ..."

"Let me finish. There is division and there is no division. All is One. The serpent swallows its tail. I am one with the Moon, and the Moon is one with the Sun, and the Sun is one with the Primordial Man, and both are one with the pure Being that sought only to Know Itself. Division and separation are how we come to know ourselves ... and when we know ourselves there is no division or separation. When you know yourself you will see this."

"I have a thousand questions ..."

"That you can answer for yourself. Questions are the desire of all being to know itself. You seek to know yourself, so know that All is One."

"When I danced with the Moon ... I danced with myself?"

"You ceased to be separate and felt the joy of union and recall."

They sat together until the Star said it was time for her to leave, for Urania would be upset if she was late.

"I thought you were not bound by time and space."

The Star laughed sweetly.

$\wp 25 \wp$

# THE END OF THE WORLD

*In which the Magician seeks the perfection of substance.*
*The Fool summons an Angel and gossips about the Devil.*
*Also some matter on Trumpets, Worlds, and their Endings.*

n her return from the West the Fool went to see the Magician. The apartment was in disarray, and the Magician
had that intense and preoccupied expression he wore when
some great project was in hand.

"What are you doing," asked the Fool.

"I seek to rectify metals and make gold," said the Magician.

"Is this not an ambition blighted with failure and ruin?"

"If you could see you would understand," said the Magician.
"Come, come!" He led her out into the alley and through a maze of
courts and passages to a small workshop.

"Gharani the goldsmith allows me the use of this space for a small
fee. He returns to his people in the South for some months. Now
witness, I have the metals. Here is copper that belongs to Venus — some
say the ore comes from the place of her birth. And lustrous tin, that is
the metal of Jupiter. And iron, that has the spirit of fierce and warlike
Mars. A flask of quicksilver for swift Mercury. Dull lead for Saturn.

And for silver these coins I won not two days ago. See how they resemble the Moon, even unto the likeness of a face. Alas, I have no gold, having spent too much in preparation, but that must soon change. Are they not marvellous in their differences?"

"Your learned eye penetrates deeper into this matter than mine."

"See, tin, soft and bright, and lead, also soft, but exceeding dull with age. Copper, reddish, and easily beaten, but tending to brittleness when worked. Iron, hard and strong, like a great warrior. And silver, akin to copper in temperament but fair and lustrous. Here you see them revealed before you in their varieties, but the Earth conceals them. The Earth conceals metals in its very substance. See this brown earth — iron. And this red earth — mercury. And this green earth — copper."

"Are these not pigments such as artisans use in the decoration of walls and the like?"

"They are, but they conceal metal. No grinding, no matter how thorough, can reveal metal — there is but a powder as you see. No metal. But heat drives out the metal, and there it is, like water from a sponge. There are great mysteries here, long concealed."

"You seek to stir my mind to comprehension, but once again you see what I do not."

"Transformation! Metamorphosis! One thing becomes another quite unlike its parent. The Earth gives birth to metals, bears them in its womb. The substance of this world is mutable, and transformed by fire. And yet there is one substance that is not mutable."

"I think you must mean gold, that resists all transformation."

"Yes! Gold is the heart of the world, the perfection of substance. All else is in some manner imperfect and corrupt. All else is debased by imperfect mixture. Copper has some of the colour but is too red, and becomes dull and tarnished. Silver has some of the lustre and is oft found with gold, for we know that Moon and Sun are often close in the sky. But alas, silver hates the touch of skin and it blackens. Lead has the softness and weight of gold but becomes grey and ugly with time. All

262

are imperfect, but Al Bharani writes that they may be cleansed of filth and dross to bring forth perfection.

"See here, I have quite degraded some iron dust from the armourer by heating it with flowers of sulphur. The bright metal is once again debased and vanished and adopts an earthy form."

"It is quite blackened, like soot."

"Quite. Now I add some vinegar."

"Oh, most vile and putrid! Quite horrid! An egg forgotten on a shelf, mixed with an outhouse in a year of the bloody flux. I must escape this stench!"

The Fool stood in the courtyard breathing fresh air. "You have devised a weapon of war. Armies could be put to rout with such a stench."

"The corruption in the heart of iron is revealed. It was concealed, like the rogue who charms with a glib tongue. If I can but cleanse substance of this vile corruption I can reveal the gold within."

"I see now this is a noble quest for a master of learning such as yourself. But you must conceal your purpose — princes might covet your secrets and put you to the question."

"Indeed, indeed. I will be discreet."

"Can you succeed where so many have failed? Can you succeed where so many have claimed success and ended their days in a cell or on the rack?"

"In every transformation, some things change, and some things stay the same. It is my unbending purpose to understand this mutability of substance and disclose the essential core, the true gold that is hidden, bright and imperishable. I see it with the eye of the mind, and it torments me beyond understanding."

"I that case I must wish you great success. I came to talk of angels. I am told I have a guiding star, and a guardian angel, and we may converse. You know of this?"

"I do. I have called on angels, and the spirits of stars and planets."

"And did they come?"

"They did come, but this world is not their abode, and they struggle to make a shape that we can perceive. Oft they talk in my mind. I thought you had direct converse with angels? I have your record written in your own hand."

"I am just returned from the far West and I am too weary to begin another journey in search of angels. I thought perhaps the angels, having wings, would make the journey in less time."

"Al Bharani speculates that angels exist *in potentia* at all places until called, and then they condense like moisture on a cold surface. And that their wings are but a fancy that denotes swiftness. And now to the matter. It is said that in the beginning, every thing was named by the First Man, and this name is the true and eternal name by which it may be called. If you know the ancient name and sign of a spirit, then you may summon it and entreat it to converse."

The Fool looked downcast. "I do not know the name of my angel. Or his sign. I neglected to ask."

"Perhaps you could call one of the princes of the angels and ask."

"I could do that?"

"Most certainly. Come, let us eat and then I will teach you the ancient name of a prince of angels."

When they had eaten and returned to the Magician's apartment, the Magician said, "I will teach you the secret name of Gabriel, who is a mighty prince of angels."

"His secret name is not Gabriel?"

"It is Gabriel, but there is a secret of articulation that is passed from master to disciple."

"You had a master?"

"When I was a youth I studied in the south with a wise student of Nature."

"What was his name?"

"His name was Ibramelekh of Khairah, but he is long dead. May we proceed?"

"Yes."

"You must learn the syllables of the name, and you must learn them separately."

"Why?"

"Is it not obvious? Because we do not wish the instantaneous presence of a prince among angels. The angels are of singular purpose and have little time for frivolous invocation. The first syllable is 'Gaa', and you must sound it like this." The Magician sang out the syllable in a clear voice. "Repeat."

The Fool copied the Magician.

"Now we must wait."

"Why?"

"Lest the syllables connect themselves together."

"They can do that?"

"Each syllable of an ancient name is one of the root sounds spoken by the Creator. They are the substance of divine agency, and come together of their own volition to make the shapes of all that exists. So we must wait lest a syllable finds its partners."

"There are arcane mysteries in being a Magician."

"There are. Bring me that sand timer."

So the Magician taught the Fool the correct way to pronounce the name of the angel, using the sand timer to ensure that the syllables were too isolated in time to ever find each other and self-assemble. The true secret name sounded like 'Gabriel', but with a some eccentric ululations on the vowels.

"And you have to draw out the final 'l' ... make it last."

"I think I have it."

"Now that you have the name, you must find a place and make it holy."

"How may I do that?"

"You must draw a circle on the earth to show you have set apart the place, and cleanse it with fire and water and salt. Then you must perfume it with sweet incense, for angels need a substance to form a body in this world. Then you should bless the spot to sanctify it and make it holy, and then you may pronounce the name."

"Is this not the work of a priest."

"In this matter you must be your own priest."

The Fool went some leagues into the countryside to the ruins of a forgotten chapel that was remote from neighbours. She pulled up weeds, swept the flagstones clear with a broom of hazel twigs, and drew a circle with a lump of chalk. She mixed salt and water and blessed it as the Magician had instructed, and sprinkled it at the four quarters, saying "By all that is holy I purify this place with salt and water." She took a burning brand around the quarters, saying "With this sacred fire I consecrate this place to the service of the Sun." She cast incense on her fire, and said the secret name. The angel came.

"You are the mighty archangel Gabriel?"

"I am. What is your purpose?"

"To converse. My feet are weary from journeys, and yet there is still much I would like to know. The Star advised me to talk to my angel, and yet I do not know his name or sign."

"The Star? I know her well."

"How do I know you are not a wicked spirit sent to mislead? The priests say the Devil sends evil spirits to deceive those who employ the arts of magic."

"The Devil, with whom you are well acquainted, is not in contention for your soul and offers no mischief. Indeed, he is curious about you, and follows your journeys with interest. Much has occurred since the world was made, and he is afflicted with Sloth, as you will know, and he fails to attend to much that is happening. For once he is intrigued and pays attention; he finds you entertaining."

XX THE ANGEL

©C.A.L. 2016

"You know the Devil? And you are not wicked or misleading?"

"We all know the Devil. He is that afflicted portion of our Lord the Sun that desires to be free of the tedium of his creation. There is likewise an element of that division in every angel, and so I have a twin who is my contrary."

"An evil spirit! So it is true! The Devil rules the legions of Hell, as the priests say."

"There is no Hell as the priests say," sighed Gabriel. "Hell is contrary spirits, and having to be nice to them."

"When I talked to the Devil he said he was going to end the world."

"He does like to say that. The injustice of Necessity, the tedium of being confined in such a contemptible little world?"

"He does seem restless and unhappy. He wants to destroy the Great North Tower and let in the powers of Chaos."

"He has a flair for drama."

"Could he do it?"

"Of course."

"Can you not stop him?"

"I have not been assigned the task. It is my unique task to signal the consummation of an age and the end of a world. I have this excellent trumpet, as you can see."

"And so you also desire to end the world!"

"Yes and no ... not as you understand it. A world ends when its confines are breached."

"Like destroying the North Tower! I don't want chaos! I like the world!"

"Your alarm and agitation is ill-conceived. I am not the herald of Chaos as you wrongly assume. As for the Devil, he has expressed the same unruly sentiments since the Sun first separated light from darkness. Just as the Sun is harmonious and unconflicted and purposeful, so the Devil is a mixture of unharmonious purposes that thwart each other. His threats of destruction and chaos would seem to account for little more than noise."

The angel continued. "This is what I perceive: the Devil, being contrary, hates the world. His hate defines his existence. His hatred is a prison, and it is a small and inclement prison, and so he hates the world all the more. Because he hates the world he is impotent to improve it for the better, and he will not admit the beauty that you can perceive. To free himself he would have to let go of his hate. This he cannot do, for he is contrary and defined by his tempers. He loves to fume and make noise. And so his world becomes yet smaller and with his whole being he desires to destroy the prison he has made for himself. He imagines he will then be free."

"He seems so smart and powerful."

"But he cannot see himself — that is his affliction. He cannot know himself."

"But we can."

"Yes."

"His world of hatred is small and he suffers. I feel so sorry for him. Can we not help him?"

"He sees that we are all stupid and blind."

"Ah," said the Fool. "He sees things he thinks *we* cannot see, and we see things we *know* he cannot see."

"Now you understand. His world is confined, and he does not see it. And that is my task, to wake up those who are confined, that they may end their worlds."

"And you have attempted this?"

"Of course. I blew my trumpet till the Sun and Moon begged me to stop. The Devil thinks he has all the best tunes."

"Ah. Yes. That."

It was at this point the Fool realised that she had neglected the simplest of courtesies.

"Would you like to sit? I have a little food and drink I can offer you."

"We do not eat; we are sustained by divine influx. But thank you for the courtesy. The incense is very fine."

"There is a little shop next to the Great Temple. I am glad you like it. I had a choice of five and I spent an age choosing. So you wake people up?"

"That is my assigned role. The Sun realised that if the world was to be governed by Necessity, that beings in the world would forget their true nature and be confined to some narrow existence."

"Ah ... ah! I see! Our vision is confined by what we have become. All beings in this world of Necessity have a narrow view, and evil is a narrow view yet more confined by self-interest and desire!"

"You have it. And now your world is already expanded."

This insight overwhelmed the Fool. The angel waited, fingering his trumpet, which of course had no valves, being what is called a natural or fanfare trumpet.

"So what happens when you blow your trumpet and someone wakens?"

"They find themselves in a new, larger world. They can see that their old world was a small world."

"And when do you sound your trumpet?"

"When it is time obviously."

"And every person is in their own small world? And they can leave it and enter a new world? There must be lots of worlds."

"There is an uncountable myriad. Come and I will show you."

In the blink of an eye they were in a vast space filled with worlds. The worlds looked like circle-crosses in a boundless grid that stretched in all directions. The angel took down a world and gave it to the Fool to hold.

"So this is a world?"

"Complete and entire."

"It does not look like much."

"They never do. It is not until you go inside that they become a world. A book does not look like much until you open the pages and begin to read."

"So what is this one?"

"It is the world of a woman in love. She thinks of nothing but the reciprocity of affection."

"He loves me, he loves me not. Yes. And this one?"

"It is the world of a man who hunts. He is consumed by the chase. He thinks of nothing else."

"So how do they work?"

"The cross you see is the four great powers that pull nothingness apart to create a world at the centre of the cross. From the inside they look like Four Watchtowers, and four mighty living beings that ward the quarters. The circle is the Ring-Pass-Not. It is an absolute barrier to causation. From the inside of a world it seems as if there is nothing beyond. It is complete and entire."

"I was told the ring was broken by the Devil."

"You call this ring the Great Serpent, the Serpent that bites its tail. Would you like to try a world?"

"Why not?"

"You might die before you are released. It is an occupational hazard."

"But do you not sound your trumpet to release me?"

"Only when you awaken and know you are confined. Then you may summon me."

"Is there a safe word?"

"My secret name."

"I will try to remember."

"I hope that you will. It becomes easier with practice."

Some time passed. An angel blew his horn, and the Fool reappeared.

"That was so intense! It all seemed so real. I completely forgot about everything. I was a Fool again, but an even bigger Fool than I am here. And then I felt the Devil in me and it was all too small and I had to get out."

"That sounds right. And was the Tower blasted?"

"Yes, that is what woke me up. My world seemed to fall apart, and I was in despair, but then I remembered your secret name. I called on you, and you blew your trumpet. Was that you?"

"There are a few of us. Would you like to try another world?"

"Most certainly. I have had much practice with being a Fool. Can I be the High Priestess? Or the Empress?"

"With regret I must tell you that you that you will begin as a Fool. That is the way it works. Fool is mandatory."

"Okay, let's do it."

# $\wp 26\wp$

# MIRANDA'S DREAM

*In which our Fool awakens to yet another, stranger dream.*

he Fool said the Angel's secret name, and the Angel came. "I am ready," she said, "You may blow your trumpet." "Are you certain?" "I am certain."

So the Angel blew his trumpet, and a new and larger world was revealed, and the old world was diminished to its true proportions.

"We were all just a pack of cards!"

"I wanted to tell you."

"I doubt that I would have understood."

"The faculty of understanding is much diminished in dream," said the Angel. "Hark, a footstep! I must depart."

Enter PROSPERO.

PROSPERO: "Awake, dear heart, awake! Thou hast slept well; Awake!"
MIRANDA: "The strangeness of your story put heaviness in me."
PROSPERO: "Shake it off. Come on, we'll visit Caliban my slave, who never yields us kind answer."

# Postscript

*In which the author no longer Plays the Fool.*
*"Knowing I loved my books,*
*he furnish'd me from mine own library*
*with volumes that I prize above my Dukedom."*
*Shakespeare, The Tempest*

There are two important intuitions that have guided the structure of this Fool's story. The first I did not intend and it emerged spontaneously in the telling. The second, which concerns the organisation of the Trump cards, is better known and is recognised by a number of authors.

The first intuition is the division between Sun and Moon, and I have followed a tradition that can be traced back to the myths of Greece and Rome. In this tale the Sun represents the social sphere, the ordering of society, and the divine institution of kingship. It represents the conscious mind and the primacy of reason. I have linked this to the Roman cult of *Sol Invictus* (the invincible or unconquerable Sun), where the Emperor was both divine and the divine proxy of the Sun on Earth.

This cult was particularly linked to Constantine (272-337 CE), who was also the first Roman Emperor to adopt Christianity as the state religion. It was Constantine who decreed a day of rest, *dies Solis*, or Sunday. In contradiction to the facts, I have assumed that Constantine did *not* adopt Christianity. In my tale the pre-Christian solar cult developed over time into a social structure not unlike medieval Christianity

— it is a counterfactual world in which the cult of *Sol Invictus* continued into the Renaissance.

The Moon represents the domestic sphere, women, and the primacy of feeling, intuition and imagination. It also stands for a world outside of the social sphere, and hence a domain that is wild, untamed, uncontrolled and perhaps threatening. Until about a hundred years ago the social sphere was primarily the domain of men (as it still is in many parts of the world). The world of the Fool depicted here is more liberal in this respect, and women have equal place (and that is why the Princess of Staves is riding a horse, and not the Prince).

The duality between Sun and Moon in the Celestial Sphere is reflected down onto some of the lower-numbered Trumps. The eighteenth century French author Antoine Court de Gébelin asserted (wrongly) that the Tarot came from Egypt, and so the male Pope was re-titled The Hierophant, and the female Pope (or Papesse) was re-titled The High Priestess. This idea has endured through many modern Tarot decks. The Hierophant thus became the high priest of an ancient *solar* religion. Likewise, in many modern Tarot decks the High Priestess has an explicit lunar association; for example, in the popular Waite/Colman Smith pack she has a crescent Moon at her feet.

The split between Sun and Moon is also partially mirrored in the duality between Emperor and Empress. The Emperor administers, while the Empress cares. The Emperor is proxy for the Sun in the secular sphere, as the Hierophant is in the religious sphere. I have assumed an identity between the crown of kingship and the *corona radiata* of later Roman Emperors — that is, I view the halo of solar radiance around the head of the Sun as the origin for the golden crown of kings. This can be seen in the illustration for the King of Coins: on the ceiling above the King of Coins there is a painting of a seated figure on a chariot with a *corona radiata* around his head. Although Renaissance Europe was Christian, a memory of the earlier cult of the Sun was retained both in popular culture and in the Tarot, and surfaced overtly when Louis

XIV of France adopted the Sun as his symbol and the sobriquet "the Sun King".

The Empress is usually taken to represent fertility, abundance, and the traditional attributes of the Mother, represented in antiquity by Aphrodite (Venus), and in particular, by the cult of Isis. The symbolism can still be found in the various cults of the Blessed Virgin Mary.

The most primal aspect of the duality of Sun and Moon is found in the Lovers. At the time of the Renaissance the raw power of attraction, *Eros*, was seen to have a cosmic and spiritual dimension, and this figures prominently in the writing of important figures such as Ficino, Dante and Boccaccio.

Duality makes a surprise appearance in the Devil, whom I have taken to be the antithesis of the Sun (and there are ancient traditions for this), and the Star, who is the complement of the Moon. Also the Devil and the Hermit, with their respective allegiances to Sin and to Virtue.

If the first intuition behind this tale concerns the primacy of Sun and Moon as an interpretative metaphor, the second concerns the internal structure of the Trumps. Many writers have tried to make sense out of the order of the Trumps. Some writers have viewed the conventional Tarot Trumps as comprising three heptads — that is, three groups of seven, making twenty-one Trumps, with the Fool as an extra unnumbered card outside of the sequence, so that the Fool "has no place". This idea is not beyond criticism, because there is variation in early Tarot card sequences, but it looks attractive when one takes the Marseilles deck as a canonical sequence.

According to this idea the first seven cards signify the social sphere, with social status being trumped first by Love, and then by Fame (the Triumph, or Chariot). The second heptad signifies the soul and subjective experience (perhaps from the specific perspective of a Stoic philosopher), with a focus on maturity and later life. Here we find old age (the Hermit), the tribulations of Fate and Fortune (the Wheel), persecution

and betrayal (the Hanged Man), Death, and Virtue (Strength, Temperance and Justice). The final seven cards signify the Celestial Realm, the world beyond the human sphere, according to a world view that is part pagan and part Renaissance Christian.

This method of organising and interpreting the Trumps has been strongly influenced by the more explicit and obvious structure of the Tarocchi of Mantegna. The Mantegna deck is not a true Tarot deck (there is no evidence it was used to play games) but it does contain an

278

obvious structure. There are five groups of ten cards.

The first group of ten is a social hierarchy. The second group has Apollo and the nine Muses. The third group is that of intellectual arts and sciences. The fourth group is a selection of virtues and principles. The fifth group is the Celestial Realm. Some of these groups would seem to have a direct bearing on the structure of the Tarot Trumps, and so the organisation of Tarot Trumps into three groups of seven is plausible and instructive.

Some readers may object that I have neglected the obvious Christian eschatological significance of the final two Trump cards. The card Judgement (sometimes called The Angel) would seem to denote the day of Judgement, when the archangel Gabriel sounds the Last Trump and the dead emerge from their tombs. Likewise, there are versions of The World that would seem to represent the New Jerusalem, the world reborn, as described in the final verses of the Biblical book of *Revelation*. I have no quarrel with this.

However, that is not how it turned out in the Fool's adventures, and the Celestials told a very different (and much more gnostic) story. I did not plan this. It just happened.

The reader may be perplexed by the odd ending of this Fool's tale. The answer comes from the history of the Tarot. The earliest and most comprehensive collection of hand-painted Tarot cards was created around 1440-1450 CE for the ruling dynasty in Milan (it is often called the Visconte-Sforza collection for this reason).

The fictional Prospero, from Shakespeare's *The Tempest*, was Duke of Milan. He was deposed and exiled to a remote island by his scheming brother. It amused me to imagine that among Prospero's famous books the young and lonely Miranda discovered an original hand-painted Tarot deck, and spent time constructing imaginative stories with them, just as our Fool describes to the Queen of Staves.

# PLAYING THE FOOL

Lightning Source UK Ltd.
Milton Keynes UK
UKHW011813060120
356473UK00001B/95/P